How To Stop Brexit
(And Make Britain Great Again)

Also by Nick Clegg

Politics: Between the Extremes

How To Stop Brexit

(And Make Britain Great Again)

NICK CLEGG

THE BODLEY HEAD
LONDON

1 3 5 7 9 10 8 6 4 2

The Bodley Head, an imprint of Vintage,
20 Vauxhall Bridge Road,
London SW1V 2SA

The Bodley Head is part of the Penguin Random House group of companies
whose addresses can be found at global.penguinrandomhouse.com.

Penguin
Random House
UK

First published by The Bodley Head in 2017

www.penguin.co.uk/vintage

A CIP catalogue record for this book is available from the British Library

ISBN 9781847925237

Typeset in India by Integra Software Services Pvt. Ltd, Pondicherry

Printed and bound by Clays Ltd, St Ives plc

Penguin Random House is committed to a sustainable future for
our business, our readers and our planet. This book is made
from Forest Stewardship Council® certified paper.

All men make mistakes, but a good man yields when he knows his course is wrong ... The only crime is pride.

Sophocles

If a democracy cannot change its mind, it ceases to be a democracy.[1]

David Davis, MP, Secretary of State for Exiting the EU

Contents

Introduction

THIS BOOK WILL EXPLAIN why it makes sense for us, as a nation, to change the decision we took on 23rd June 2016 to leave the European Union. It will then explain how we can do so.

It starts from the premise that, in a free democracy, we are entitled to change our minds. We do this every day in our own lives. From taking the wrong turning in a car to accepting the wrong job or ending a failing relationship – we all make mistakes all the time. And we correct them. To err, and then change course, is human.

By contrast, an inability to change course is a restriction of liberty. How can we be free if we can't change our minds when things don't turn out as we'd hoped? There is nothing wrong with revisiting a decision, if its consequences don't match the promises made by those who advocated it. As John Maynard Keynes famously declared, 'When the facts change, I change my mind.' And the facts surrounding Brexit are radically different from the expectations raised by those who advocated it, so we have every right to change our minds.

How To Stop Brexit is not primarily aimed at those readers who are fanatically supportive of our membership of the EU or fanatically opposed to it. Nor is it intended for an expert audience well versed in the ways of Whitehall, Westminster and Brussels. It is intended mainly for those people who don't hold their views for or against Brexit especially strongly, and are prepared to think again. Some will have voted 'Remain', others for 'Brexit'. Many will have voted because they felt a duty to do so, even though they were uneasy about being asked to take such a momentous decision in the first place. Many are feeling increasingly unsettled by the political rancour and economic uncertainty that have followed the referendum, and want to know whether there is a better way forward. This is also a book addressed squarely at those many people who voted for Brexit knowing exactly what they were doing, based on the information given to them at the time, but who now see that Brexit is not turning out the way they were promised, and want to do something about it.

Whichever of these readers you might be, I want to persuade you that you have every right to think again about what we did in 2016; to take back control of your own future and to change course to restore certainty and stability to our country.

If this was little more than a book about the *Nightmare before Brexit*, then it would plunge me – and you, no doubt – into a state of despair. Instead, over the following pages I want to lift the mood. I will explain why, in view of political developments in the EU and here in the UK, there is a clear route to Britain changing its mind and putting Brexit on hold. But I want to go further still. This book proposes a number of actions that all of us, in all walks of life, can take, if we want this country to alter course. If enough people were to take these actions and stick to them, then I am sure that Brexit could be stopped.

Whether you voted Remain or Leave, or not at all, on 23rd June, *How To Stop Brexit* will give you a new-found determination to challenge the anger, vitriol and pessimism that have engulfed our country in the wake of the Brexit vote. Once you turn the final page you will, I hope, feel emboldened and confident that we can take a better decision about the future of our country.

You can stop Brexit. You can help lead Britain towards a new, settled status within a reformed European Union. You can reject the debilitating and poisonous politics of Westminster. You can help give our young people what they crave – an open-minded and open-hearted Britain. You can help Britain be a leader in Europe, and the world, again.

In short, to borrow a well-worn phrase, you can help make Britain great again.

There is a silver lining to Brexit

AT THE ENGLISH CHANNEL'S narrowest point, just over eighteen nautical miles separate Shakespeare Beach in Kent from Cap Gris Nez, and on a clear day you can stand on the British shoreline, peer across the waves and make out the French coastline. Yet the reality is that we are in many ways a country far apart from our continental cousins, with this small stretch of sea representing more than a mere geographical separation. There is a psychological distance, a belief that the British Isles are a long way removed from the many nations with which we share the European hemisphere. We are an island nation, with an island outlook on the world. Yet just at the point that Brexit appears to make us more of an island than ever, it could paradoxically lead to changes in the EU that will offer us a way back in.

Our history weighs heavily, subconsciously perhaps, on how we feel about our place in the world. For more than a thousand years Britain has often viewed the rest of Europe with a mixture of affection, fear and suspicion. Frequently it has been the home of our enemy, with these islands fighting long wars with France, Spain, Tsarist Russia and Germany. A long roll-call of battles is etched permanently into our national historical memory: Agincourt, Blenheim, Waterloo, Dunkirk, the Battle of Britain. This focus on our military past reinforces the feeling of British exceptionalism. Since 1066, no foreign force has successfully managed to cross the Channel and launch a full-scale invasion and conquest of these isles. No other nation on the continent can say the same.

The sense of separation runs deeper still. We have gone it alone before when, in 1534, Henry VIII split from the Catholic Church and defied the authority of the Pope. The defence of our newly established Anglicanism – always under threat, real or imagined, from the forces of Rome and the Catholic nations of Europe – embedded itself in the national psyche.

In the eighteenth century we then took our continental rivalry across the world, as Britain, fuelled by the Industrial Revolution, pieced together a vast empire, and our European neighbours sought to build their own imperial spheres of influence.

As British forces fought side-by-side with our European neighbours in the two world wars of the twentieth century, the sense of Britain being somehow separate – even superior – was enhanced. Until the United States came to our aid, we were a nation that, in our darkest hour, had to rely on itself. 'We stand alone in the breach,' declared Winston Churchill in the summer of 1940. More than three-quarters of a century since Britain helped lead the allied nations to victory against Hitler's Nazi forces, many people believe that Britain still stands alone today.

This awareness of our history, and the peculiar mix of superiority and separateness that it has spawned, played a vital role in Britain's decision to stay out of the earliest attempts at European integration. Upon the creation of the European Coal and Steel Community in 1951, Jean Monnet, one of its founders, reflected on Britain's refusal to take part. 'I never understood why the British did not join,' Monnet noted. 'I came to the conclusion that it must have been because it was the price of victory – the illusion that you could maintain what you had, without change.'

By the 1960s, however, a reluctant acceptance that Britain *had* to change had set in. Post-imperial

Britain was no longer as powerful on the world stage, and we grudgingly accepted that it was time to seek more than simply a stand-off role in Europe.

With that mindset, it is not surprising that there was little fanfare when we finally made the leap and joined this growing European club. Instead, the nation gave a collective shrug of its shoulders. 'We're In – but Without Fireworks,' declared *The Guardian*, as Britain formally joined the European Economic Community (EEC) on 1st January 1973. In fact there was barely a sparkler to be seen. Basic economic necessity, rather than ideology, hope or inspiration, lay behind Britain's decision to end the country's splendid isolation. In the early 1970s the economy of Britain was in poor health. Unemployment was at its highest since the 1930s. The government was embroiled in endless battles with powerful trade-union leaders. And on the international stage, just twenty-five years after the Royal Navy had helped to win the Second World War, Britain was losing out in a series of disputes over North Sea fishing rights – the so-called 'Cod Wars' – to teeny Iceland. The sick man of Europe was in a critical condition. Britain looked on with envy (and some desperation) as the economies of the six founder members of the EEC, formed with the signing of the Treaty of Rome in 1957, grew far faster than our own. As the empire fell away, as the Commonwealth struggled to compete and Britain's global influence receded, we sought belated entry into this successful, embryonic European club.

If we want to understand Brexit today, we need to acknowledge the distinct circumstances in which we joined the European club in the first place. Our original decision was shaped by a sense of national decline. That pessimism stood in stark contrast to the more positive motives of other EU member states. For France and Germany and the other founding member states (Belgium, Italy, Luxembourg and the Netherlands), taking the first steps towards European partnership was a way of proving that war would not ravage the continent again; that lasting peace finally beckoned. For Spain (which found its initial attempt to join the EEC rejected, because of objections to Franco's authoritarian rule), EEC membership, when it finally came in 1986, was a symbol of democracy's victory over fascism. And for the many central and eastern European nations that began the process of applying for membership after the fall of the Berlin Wall in 1989, becoming part of the EU was a demonstration of their new-found freedom from the grip of Soviet-era communism. In all these cases, formally agreeing to work with European neighbours, to build partnerships and to strengthen institutional and economic ties was both a symbolic and a practical step towards a brighter and better future. Membership of the European club said something big and positive about these countries' own national identity.

For Britain, in contrast, membership was a half-hearted punt that we might be able to reduce the price of butter, with the 1975 referendum on our membership of the EEC a dry affair which made appeals to people's wallets rather than their hearts. Not surprisingly, we have been rather ambivalent about the whole project ever since. Our decision to join was never cemented by a positive statement in favour of our European identity. Pulse-racing pro-European rhetoric has been notably absent from British public life. Predictably, then, during the 2016 referendum the Remain campaign found that its somewhat mundane focus on the economic reasons for EU membership was often drowned out by the Leave campaign's emotional evocation of an age of empire and of glories past and stolen.

Despite these constant reservations about our role in the EU, over the last forty years Britain has played a pivotal role in shaping its development and design. A mixture of foot-dragging, brazen self-confidence and pernickety attention to the small print has frequently been a source of intense annoyance to our European partners, but once we'd secured a seat at the table, Britain made sure that our voice was heard and our weight was thrown around to good effect. We may have been a late entry into the EEC, but we soon became one of its most influential members.

So it is sad to watch the Euroscepticism that has gripped the leaderships of both the Labour and the Conservative parties overlook our achievements in Europe. Over the last four decades, in countless election manifestos, Britain's two largest political parties have repeatedly boasted about their ability to set the agenda in the EU – and they were right to do so. British governments, whether they were Labour or Conservative, have led the way in reform of the Common Fisheries and Common Agricultural policies, in the forging of common EU foreign-policy approaches, in cross-border cooperation against terrorism and crime, in opening up international trade, in pioneering new environmental protections, in enforcing better budgetary and administrative housekeeping, and in leading the case for the expansion of the EU after the collapse of Soviet communism.

Most important of all – though Brexiteers pretend this isn't the case – Margaret Thatcher was pivotal in the creation of the Single Market itself, the world's most sophisticated and complete barrier-less marketplace. They replay her 1988 speech in Bruges in which she rejected 'a European super-state exercising a new dominance from Brussels', and they quote her 1990 performance in the House of Commons when she dismissed calls for greater central control in Europe with a theatrical 'no, no, no'. And after basking in the Iron Lady's YouTube highlights, they insist that she would be at the forefront of the Brexit campaign. They are wrong to do so: my guess is that she would be unsettled by their reckless drive to pull Britain out of *her* Single Market. Thatcher urged British business to embrace this new open market with a 'positive attitude of mind' and to throw themselves into the 'direct and unhindered access to the purchasing power of over 300 million of the world's wealthiest and most prosperous people'.[2] How baffling that so many of her devoted acolytes seem to have forgotten their heroine's advice.

Mrs Thatcher was even happy to speak in French on occasion, when required. But she needn't have bothered, because English, over time, established itself as the main language in which the European Union conducts its business. Until the 1990s it was French, one of the twenty-four official languages of the EU, that was the dominant language in the Brussels institutions. As the EU expanded, new additions such as Sweden and Finland were far more inclined to use English as their second language, a trend that was repeated when the central and eastern European nations joined the EU. Today English is by far the most common language used in the EU institutions and dominates debate amongst Members of the European Parliament. Even when we're not trying, our influence in Europe has grown.

So while we may not be entirely comfortable inside the EU, and may see ourselves as a nation apart, we have, repeatedly, shaped its priorities and direction. Time and again, Britain's unsettled relationship with Europe has prompted us to seek a series of special deals. And guess what? Time and again, Britain has succeeded in carving out a special status for itself. Did we join the eurozone? Are we part of the border-free Schengen Area? Did we sign up to all 130 of the EU's Justice and Home Affairs laws? No. No. No. Margaret Thatcher would have liked the sound of that. Along with Denmark, we were one of just two countries not to adopt the euro, or be legally bound to do so, at the time it was launched. Bulgaria, Croatia, Cyprus, Ireland and Romania are the only other EU nations to have opted out of Schengen. And the UK has, with Denmark and Ireland, secured a deal whereby it can opt in or out of legislation relating to freedom, justice and security, on a case-by-case basis.

And when it comes to financial contributions to the EU, the UK is alone in securing a permanent reduction to the contributions that it makes. It was Margaret Thatcher, a year before her crucial endorsement of the Single Market, who, in 1984, secured this unique deal for Britain. The argument was multi-pronged, but centred on the assertion that the UK, with a relatively small number of farms, was receiving a proportionately small share of the farm subsidies that accounted for around 70 per cent of EU expenditure. When the British Prime Minister complained that Britain was the victim of a skewed arrangement, the rest of the EU eventually, if a little grumpily, agreed with her. Since then, the UK's cashback deal has seen it reclaim a substantial chunk of the sum it sends to Brussels: the rebate, worth around £4.5 billion in

2016,[3] has seen more than £85bn returned to the UK since 1985.[4] Not surprisingly, there are plenty in the EU who resent having to send their own money to the UK, and plenty who would gladly rip up an arrangement that Tony Blair described as an 'anomaly'.

It is worth repeating the uniqueness of the situation: we are, or were, the one nation to receive such a rebate on a permanent basis, and everyone, from the richest EU nations like Germany to the poorer member states like Bulgaria and Romania, contributes to our tailor-made deal.

Within the intricate stitching that binds the EU, there is a common thread that runs throughout: Britain's unique status. Far from being the inflexible, homogenous monolith of *Daily Mail* caricature, the European Union has repeatedly shown that it is willing to listen, prepared to compromise and ready to reform. So when people like me insist that Britain can still act to further reform the EU, and help mould it in a manner that best suits this country's very specific needs, we are not in the throes of some 'remoaning' Europhile fever. We are simply stating the obvious. Britain has enjoyed a special status throughout our time as a member of the EU and, should we choose to, we could do so once again. It would be a logical continuation of what we have previously achieved on so many occasions.

Crucially, this task – of reuniting the UK with the EU, but on an altered and reformed basis – will be made all the more possible because the rest of the EU is beginning to redesign its entire structure itself. Indeed, after recent events, it has no other choice. Europe's leaders, especially in the wake of Emmanuel Macron's election as French president, are increasingly persuaded that extensive reform of the EU is now inescapable. The Brexit vote was a major catalyst in pushing EU governments to accept that change can no longer be avoided. In an ironic twist of fate, the Brexit vote in Britain against a future in the EU may help to provoke precisely the reforms that will assist in securing the EU's own future.

So there is a silver lining to the Brexit referendum: it may help to strengthen the EU itself; and it may lead to the conditions in which the UK could be reintegrated into a reformed EU.

To say that the EU has been going through something of a rocky time in recent years is an understatement. Go back to the summer of 2015 and ask a random person in the street what they associate with the EU, and it would not be peace and prosperity. Most likely there would be two answers: uncontrolled borders and economic hardship.

It is easy to see why the EU became associated with the uncontrolled movement of people. Ever since the Treaty of Rome established the European Economic Community in 1957, the project has held the free movement of people to be a good in itself. Dismantling barriers to the free exchange of capital, goods and services went hand-in-hand with the ability of European citizens to choose where in the EU they wanted to live and work. In this way the obstacles to trade and commerce across national borders would be dissolved, a European marketplace would emerge, and greater understanding would be fostered on a continent scarred by centuries of conflict.

For many years the numbers of people taking advantage of this right were small, perhaps because the early member states of the EU were all relatively well off. But as the Union enlarged, a number of poorer Mediterranean countries and, later, former Soviet-bloc countries joined. Average wages in countries like Poland and Romania were far lower than they were in the west and the north (though they were, and are, catching up).[5] Now their highly motivated and often well-educated workers could earn more abroad than they were able to at home.

Many of them chose to exercise their new right to work in the UK. Net migration from the EU stood at 15,000 in 2003,[6] but by 2015 it was at a record 180,000.[7] In part that reflects the pace of EU expansion, with thirteen new countries joining since 2004. But it also reflects the attractiveness of the UK as a place to live and work: the relative strength of our economy throughout much of that period, the availability of jobs, wage levels that compare favourably with home countries, a tolerant and diverse culture, plus the English language ensured that the UK was a favourite destination for many European workers.

In most respects, this wave of EU immigration has been good news for the UK. The increased flow of migrant labour has suited British businesses, which would otherwise have faced skills and labour shortages in many sectors. Many firms now depend on ready access to labour from across the EU. Exhaustive studies have shown that the impact of this change on local jobs and wage levels has been small.[8] Far from driving out indigenous workers, EU migration has helped to expand our economy. Far from proving a drain on public services, EU workers have made a net contribution through their taxes.[9]

But this happened by accident rather than by design. No one was shown a plan, back in 2004, setting out the changes that would happen to our economy and our society as a result of EU enlargement. No one voted for such an outcome. Quite the opposite – a study was commissioned in 2003 that predicted that the ten countries joining the EU in 2004 would add just 13,000 a year to the UK's population.[10] On that basis, the decision was taken by the then Labour government not to impose an optional seven-year brake on the free movement of workers from the new member states. Instead we welcomed workers from Poland, the Czech Republic and elsewhere with open arms. Only the UK, Ireland and Sweden did so, while everyone else kept restrictions in place.

In hindsight, it was clearly a mistake to open our borders before the vast majority of other countries did so. It meant, for example, that tens of thousands of people who would probably have gone to Germany, France or the Benelux countries came to the UK instead. And it enabled populists like Nigel Farage to claim that the EU was the source of uncontrolled immigration. The government should have coordinated the lifting of transitional controls with those countries, to ensure that numbers were evenly distributed. That would have still given us the economic benefits, but would have allowed us to better manage the numbers who arrived.

While the decision not to impose transitional controls in 2004 lies squarely with the UK, two other momentous events outside our control helped to sharpen and toxify the immigration issue in our recent national debate.

The first was the migrant crisis in the Mediterranean. According to the International Organisation for Migration, an estimated one million refugees and economic migrants made the perilous sea crossing to enter the EU in 2015. Around half were fleeing the civil war in Syria. Nearly 4,000 people are thought to have died in the attempt. Many of those who made it headed north through the western Balkans, but found their route blocked in Hungary, whose authoritarian Prime Minister, Viktor Orbán, ordered the erection of fences along the borders with Serbia and Croatia. And so the sight of shipwrecked boats and make-shift refugee camps on our TV screens was added to the chaotic scenes of crowds of tired, hungry refugees and their children trudging from one town to the next, or desperately trying to board over-loaded trains.

The impact of these images cannot be over-stated. They linked the idea of the free movement of migrants within the EU to the idea of disorderly and uncontrolled immigration from outside the EU. And they eloquently underlined the weakness of the EU and its institutions. Instead of coming up with a joint solution to a humanitarian crisis on their own borders, Europe's nations collapsed into mutual recrimination and started erecting national borders again.

Part of the anxiety created by those scenes was a concern that among the crowds were Islamic State (IS) terrorists posing as refugees. While the chances of that were deliberately stoked by the right-wing media, it wasn't a baseless worry. Hundreds of Europeans are known to have travelled to train with and fight for so-called Islamic State in Syria, and IS had made it known that they were seeking to carry out attacks in Europe. The risk was confirmed by the attacks in Paris on 13th November 2015, where again the fluidity of Europe's borders seemed to be at least in part to blame. Two of the attackers had entered Europe via Greece from Syria in October; all had fought for IS in Syria and had returned; the cell was based in Belgium and the attackers crossed effortlessly into France.

So a palpable sense that Europe was the cause of serious threats to our well-being and security, rather than a solution, was well and truly in the air on the eve of the referendum vote. Indeed, it has been reported that in a private conversation in the Prime Minister's flat shortly before the referendum, the pro-Brexit editor of the *Daily Mail*, Paul Dacre, pointed to a TV screen and told David Cameron that the pictures of refugees on the daily news would be the reason voters would support Brexit.[11]

Second, until very recently the health of Europe's economy has also been a cause for considerable public concern. In normal times, we might have expected people to acknowledge that even if the EU was failing to work properly in some areas, at least it provided self-evident benefits in terms of jobs, trade and prosperity. Yet since the economic crash of 2008, the EU's eurozone has stumbled from one economic crisis to the next, centred especially on the chronic weakness of the Greek economy and the cruel explosion in joblessness across southern Europe. The overwhelming impression has been of a system teetering on the edge.

Amongst Anglo-American commentators and analysts – who provide the bulk of the analysis in global financial markets – it became fashionable to predict the collapse of the euro, and the possible demise of the EU as a whole. I heard Conservative ministers around the Coalition Cabinet table loftily predict on numerous occasions that it was only a matter of time before the euro would collapse. They approached the subject with a peculiar relish, willing on an outcome without appearing to care that it would have plunged the UK economy into a deep and lengthy recession.

The immediate crisis seems to have passed. At the time of writing, the eurozone economy is growing again – considerably faster than the UK's Brexit-blighted economy – and its prospects are looking healthier. But under the surface, large question marks still remain.

The truth is that the euro-project incorporated some important weaknesses from the start. For one thing, it lacked some of the key institutions and powers that are normally associated with a currency union: yes, it established a Central Bank with decision-making powers over interest rates, but it provided little coordinated control over taxation and spending by its members. The rules that had been established at the outset to force governments to live within their means were largely ignored, not least by France and Germany. This meant that countries ended up running their particular corner of the eurozone as they saw fit, many of them spending freely and racking up unsustainable deficits. The link between interest rates and tax-and-spend – between monetary and fiscal policy – was broken.

At the same time, there were grave imbalances between members of the eurozone, which were made worse by the crash of 2008. The dominance of the German economy meant that the interest rate set by the European Central Bank tended to respond to the rhythm of the German economy, while ignoring the weaknesses and the overheating in others. A weak euro meant that Germany, as a major exporter, could sell more successfully to the rest of the world, and low interest rates helped to keep the value of the currency down. But in a currency union the same interest rate has to apply across every participating country. So low interest rates in Germany meant excessively low interest rates in Spain, Portugal and Ireland. And when those countries' economies started to overheat, their governments suddenly realised that one of their most important levers – the ability to cool the froth by raising interest rates – was no longer available to them. And so the bubbles continued to grow; households borrowed and bought too much, a construction boom spiralled out of control, debts continued to mount and, when the banking sector imploded in 2008, the artificially inflated growth in large parts of the eurozone collapsed, unemployment sky-rocketed and, by 2010, a number of countries were asking for international help.

As a result, the economic storm since 2008 has left the eurozone badly divided between the wealthy 'creditor' countries of the north and the struggling 'debtor' countries of the south. The north has found itself on the hook, forced to bail out banks in the south that are running low on capital, and to lend large sums of money to governments whose creditworthiness is such that they can no longer borrow unaided on the international markets.

These are all serious problems. It is unsurprising, therefore, that voters in the UK looked across the Channel and recoiled at what they saw: people didn't want to be yoked to a club of nations which they were told was synonymous with uncontrolled immigration, security threats and the risk that British taxpayers might have to pay to rescue other countries from the economic abyss. All of this compelled us to think again about the UK's relationship with the EU.

So the big question is this: just how can the EU redesign itself to address these weaknesses in a way that works for everyone, including the UK?

For far too long Europe's leaders have ducked the inevitable need to revisit the institutional architecture – by way of yet another revision of the EU's founding treaties – that governs the core economic and currency union at the heart of the EU.

To be fair, in 2011 they did propose some new rule changes to stabilise the ailing eurozone, but David Cameron ended up vetoing it in December of that year because it didn't give him the concessions he believed he needed, in order to satisfy his party. Not that it changed anything – Britain was simply sidestepped, and the rest of the EU went ahead anyway with their own 'intergovernmental' deal – a treaty outside the formal structures of the EU. After that painful experience, France and Germany were adamant that there would be no new treaties, and that the eurozone crisis would be addressed using the treaty powers already available. The threat of the UK hijacking a formal process and turning it into a stage for the Conservative Party's internal battles was too much.

Yet without a new treaty, the EU has had to muddle through with piecemeal change that falls short of the fundamental reform that circumstances

demand. The single-currency area is healing, but
the eurozone crisis revealed deep economic tensions
that must be resolved if the EU is to avoid similar
problems in future. The eurozone will need to integrate much more closely, accepting a larger degree
of centralised control to ensure greater fiscal disci-
pline, leading in the longer term to a smoothing
out of the major disparities in Gross Domestic
Product (GDP) per capita and productivity. In
return, the weaker economies will expect sustained
support from the larger, wealthier economies.

Some of this is already happening: new powers
have been introduced to supervise eurozone banks
and to rescue them if they fail; a €500bn bailout
fund has been established to provide loans to countries in economic distress; and a more activist
European Central Bank is now willing to use its
capital to buy government debt and stimulate
economic activity.[12] But a strategic vision to bring
the eurozone closer together has been lacking.
Until now.

Finally, with Brexit removing the UK from the
picture, and with Emmanuel Macron's election
bringing a new spirit of optimism to continental
politics, the possibility of 'more Europe' is firmly
back on the agenda. The long-dormant Franco-
German engine of the EU has spluttered back to

life. Meeting Macron the day after his inauguration, Angela Merkel declared that both were willing to entertain treaty change in order to implement a 'road map … [for] how we can deepen the existing European Union and especially the euro zone'.[13]

This changes everything. There is now explicit recognition that, without London at the table, Paris and Berlin must exercise leadership. As Macron said on the campaign trail, 'since 2008 we have failed to build Europe. Since 2008 we have had a lost generation that has seen only a vacuum of plans. Our duty is to rebuild the European dream.'[14]

It isn't solely about the money, of course. Recent events have also made the EU as a whole more sensitive to public concerns about the mass movement of people and the threat of terrorism and cross-border crime. Just as Britain has argued about how best to take back control of its own borders, so the EU has struggled to find a solution to manage its own. As more than a million migrants flooded into mainland Europe in 2015, EU nations fell out with each other as they sought to stem the flow. Some countries tried to divert the migrant routes; others made clear that, contrary to pleas from Brussels, the migrants would be turned away. Slovenia erected a razor-wire fence along its border with Croatia. Austria constructed a 2.3-mile barrier along its border with Slovenia – the first fence between two Schengen Area countries. Hungary closed its border with Croatia; Slovakia followed by shutting its border with Hungary. Concrete and barbed-wire barriers are now part of the EU map, a design feature that was never part of the blueprint for a harmonious union of nations.

The EU has responded by agreeing a faintly grubby deal with Turkey: Ankara has been handed a cool €3bn (£2.3bn) to help the estimated 2.7 million Syrians now stuck on Turkish soil, and a promise to speed up Turkish visa applications, in return for Turkey taking back thousands of migrant asylum-seekers who have landed in Greece.[15] It is a rather desperate, sticking-plaster solution. Leading EU politicians are all too aware that there has been a huge design flaw in the EU, and that removing internal borders within the Schengen Area – while failing to fix external ones — is not working. Different countries require different approaches to their borders, depending in large part on their proximity to the Mediterranean refugee crisis. Just as Britain is full of angst about the movement of people within the EU, so the EU is grappling with the issue of the movement of people into the EU.

*

So how might a reformed EU actually look? Back in December 2011, as Whitehall's top brass sat around digesting the fallout from Cameron's surprise veto of the EU's draft treaty, I remember there was a lot of talk about the EU developing into a series of 'concentric circles' – a kind of hub-and-spoke arrangement – in which the eurozone formed the hub and Britain was located in an outer circle, a spoke-length away from the inner core. The thing we all realised at the time was that the EU countries that shared the single currency were obliged to move ahead at pace to overcome the economic crisis, leaving the non-eurozone members of the EU, and in particular Britain, behind.

While this may all sound pretty uncontroversial and obvious – how else was the eurozone going to survive? – in truth it represented a final departure from the ideology of an 'ever-closer union', which had loosely governed the EC and then the EU ever since the 1950s; a belief that in the end all the member states were destined for the same distant horizon. The eurozone crisis led to a clear and overt recognition that the nations of Europe were not all embarked on the same journey, and that some of them circled each other in distinctly different orbits.

Yet there was an immediate problem. The eurozone countries now formed their own natural club-within-a-club, and because of the voting rules in the European Council, this eurozone club would have an automatic majority in all the key votes. In government, we realised there was now a risk that on occasion there might be circumstances in which they might use that majority to change the rules of the Single Market in a way that suited them, but didn't necessarily suit us. And there was nothing we could do about it, because Cameron's 'veto' had just rendered us marginal in the discussions on the eurozone's future. So we were faced with the tricky dilemma of being by far the largest EU member state not to be in the eurozone, but at the same time being at risk of being outvoted on core EU business by eurozone member states. A new, explicitly differentiated approach to membership of the EU was fast becoming imperative.

The idea of a multi-speed Europe (going at different paces to roughly the same destination) or an EU of concentric circles (some integrating further and deeper than others) is not new. It has been around since at least 1975, when a report by former Belgian Prime Minister Leo Tindemans declared that 'it is impossible at the present time to submit a credible programme of action [for European integration] if it is deemed absolutely necessary that in every case all stages should be reached by all the States at the same time'. In 1994, the Prime Minister of France, Édouard Balladur, proposed that the EU should be made up of three concentric circles: an inner core of the single currency, a middle tier of those in the EU but not in the single currency, and an outer circle of non-members with close links to the EU. Since then, various prominent European politicians have put forward proposals to formalise what rapidly became the practical reality: some countries were ready and willing to move faster or integrate deeper than others.

Of course in many ways the UK's pre-Brexit status suggested that the EU had already developed the art of differential integration, notwithstanding the customary lip-service paid to the ethos of 'ever-closer union'. We are in the Single Market, but not in the euro; in the common security and defence arrangements, but not in the Schengen borderless area; in many of the police and crime-fighting measures, but out of a large number of them. And we are not alone in wanting to pick and choose: of the twenty-seven EU member states (minus the UK), twenty-one are in Schengen, and nineteen in the euro (though those who are out of the euro are almost all expected to join, eventually).

The idea of formalising this state of affairs is once again in the air. In August 2016 the influential Brussels-based think tank Bruegel published a paper calling for a 'continental partnership' – a new form of 'outer circle' for a post-Brexit UK and other non-EU countries that want to belong to the Single Market and have some say over its rules, but want to control the free movement of citizens and don't want to play a part in the political institutions of the Union.[16] And in March 2017, to coincide with the sixtieth anniversary of the founding Treaty of Rome, the European Commission published a document setting out five scenarios for the future of the EU, one of which imagined sub-groups of member states pursuing their own integration agendas, ranging from defence to policing.[17]

Both Angela Merkel and Emmanuel Macron have called for a 'multi-speed Europe', in recognition of the fact that the eurozone now needs to take steps that will be unpalatable to other countries. As Macron has put it, 'If the eurozone has not made progress in recent years it is because it is ashamed of itself and because it is afraid to face up to those that preferred to stay on the balcony or in the entrance hall.'[18]

So the notion of redrawing the political geography of the EU to better accommodate its diversity is an old idea whose time has come. Should we want to, the opportunity exists for Britain to carve out a new relationship with the continent that better reflects our distinctive preferences. There will be a Europe of concentric circles. Through ingenuity and generosity, we could find, if we chose to, a place for Britain within this new EU.

If the triple-whammy of the eurozone economic crisis, the refugee crisis and Brexit were the immediate catalysts prompting the European Union to focus on the need for reform, the sucker punch of Donald Trump's presidential victory stunned it into even more urgent action.

Brexit, followed by Trump's self-proclaimed 'Brexit plus plus plus' victory, had excitable pundits predicting that an unstoppable right-wing populist surge was poised to sweep across the whole of Europe. There had been a dramatic shift in the political weather; could Europe survive the coming storm?

The answer, it appears, is a resounding Yes. By the Christmas after the Brexit referendum, the clouds had already begun to lift. In Austria, the pro-European Alexander Van der Bellen defeated Norbert Hofer's far-right Freedom Party

and issued a warning against the dangers of falling
into 'nationalism and small-country parochialism'.
In Britain, the populists reacted with customary
grace. Responding to what he called the wrong
result, Arron Banks, the man who bankrolled
the campaign to leave the EU, tweeted that the
Austrian electorate 'haven't suffered enough rape
and murder yet'.[19]

The Brexiteers then predicted that the
Netherlands would topple next. 'We may well be
close, perhaps, to a Nexit,' Nigel Farage confidently
opined on the morning after the referendum.[20] In
March 2017, Mark Rutte – the leader of the liberal
VVD party – comfortably defeated the right-wing
populist Geert Wilders, who had been leading in
the polls for the best part of two years. 'This was
an evening when ... the Netherlands said "Stop" to
the wrong sort of populism,' Rutte declared.

In neighbouring France, Marine Le Pen, leader
of the far-right Front National, had predicted that
2017 would be the year in which 'the peoples of
Continental Europe wake up'. In May, however, she
was well beaten by the centrist Emmanuel Macron,
a proud Europhile who vowed, upon his victory, that
'we have never needed Europe more'.

The populists all shared the same angry
message. Trump promised, ever more frantically, to

'make America great again'. Farage issued a battle cry of 'we want our country back'. Le Pen vowed to 'give France back its Freedom'. The Austrian Freedom Party's slogan was 'Austria first'. And all have expressed their admiration for Vladimir Putin's authoritarian brand of leadership in Russia.

For now, however, Europe appears to be resistant to populism's seductive appeal. The reasons behind the recent run of election results require extensive analysis, but it is clear that the shock of Brexit, followed by Trump's victory, inspired liberal-minded, internationalist, pro-European politicians to come out of their shells and make their arguments with renewed passion. They can no longer close their eyes and pretend there is no populist threat. They can no longer assume that we have reached, as the political scientist Francis Fukuyama famously stated, the end of history. Instead they have had to take their message to voters – many of whom are unhappy with the status quo – with fresh arguments and a promise to listen and reform. Europe has been shocked into action and is determined to ... well, make Europe great again.

The Times is often credited with a headline that, sadly, never actually appeared. 'Dense Fog in the Channel: Continent Isolated' is such a perfect description of British attitudes towards Europe that it turns out it was too good to be true. But while the fog over the Channel might sometimes appear to be thicker than ever, it is in fact beginning to lift. Look closer and you can begin to make out the outline of a new European vessel emerging from the mist, an EU under reconstruction, which is sleeker, more nimble and perhaps more accommodating to us Brits than that which came before.

So there has been a huge amount of change across Europe – and the world – in the months since our Brexit referendum. And when the world changes, people's views change, too. In this new landscape, I will now explain why stopping Brexit would not be anti-democratic. It would actually be the *more* democratic thing to do.

Why it is right to stop Brexit

THE REFERENDUM CAMPAIGN WAS, for the most part, an uninspiring affair – for which both sides must bear some responsibility. Much of the argy-bargy between the two sides was unenlightening and forgettable. Some images, however, cannot be erased. When I close my eyes and drag my mind back to those grim spring months of 2016, a red bus rolls into view and its infamous slogan blinks back at me once more: 'We send the EU £350m every week. Let's fund the NHS instead.' I'm sure you remember it all too well.

Not surprisingly, the promise of such riches for our National Health Service caught the public imagination. Boris Johnson, Michael Gove and the other leading Leave campaigners regularly appeared in front of banners that repeated the claim. Even after the UK Statistics Authority pointed out that the figure 'was misleading and undermines trust in official statistics',[21] the pledge remained plastered to the bus's side.

The Leave campaign knew that they had a potent promise on their hands, but just how crucial was the £350m claim to the final referendum result? Dominic Cummings, a one-time government adviser to Mr Gove who was later employed as the strategic mastermind of the official Leave campaign, has said, 'Would we have won without £350m/NHS? All our research and the close result strongly suggests No.'[22] More than a year on, the NHS is yet to see any of Cummings' Brexit bounty, nor will it ever do so. The economy is suffering such uncertainty after the Brexit vote that Philip Hammond, the Chancellor, has already identified – conservatively – a new £59bn black hole in the public finances,[23] money that could otherwise be spent on public services like the NHS. If we include the additional cost of replacing the thousands of doctors and nurses from across the EU who work in our NHS – many of whom have already quit, following the referendum[24] – it quickly becomes clear that our NHS is getting less, not more, money because of the Brexit vote.

It is not surprising, then, that just twenty-four hours after the referendum result, Nigel Farage, the former UKIP leader and Brexit standard-bearer in chief, admitted that he couldn't guarantee the £350m weekly windfall, adding that he 'would never have made that claim'.[25] He was quickly followed by leading Conservative Brexiteers such as Iain Duncan Smith – who campaigned in front of the red bus – and the present Brexit Secretary, David Davis, both of whom have been at pains to say that they never made such a promise. This is small comfort to the many people who voted to bring Britain out of the EU, in the belief that it would provide a much-needed injection of cash for the health service.

While the non-existent £350m per week for the NHS is the most symbolic of the Leave campaign's broken promises, it is only one of numerous decisive pledges that have failed to materialise. Michael Gove's promise that Brexit would see VAT on fuel and energy slashed, to ensure that 'bills will be lower for everyone'? Nothing so far. The commitment to restore exclusive control over British waters to British fishermen? Gove has now admitted that EU trawlers will continue to operate in UK waters.[26] A promise that immigration from the EU to the UK would be dramatically slashed? David Davis has now confessed that immigration from the EU will in fact rise 'from time to time'.[27] A new, Australian-style immigration points system, as promised by Gove and Johnson as they attacked their own government's approach towards immigration as 'completely out of control'? Rejected by their own government. The eighty million Turks who, we were told, were likely to 'flood' into the UK, if we voted to Remain? By and large, they've remained in Turkey. Tight control over British borders? It now appears there won't be any controls monitoring people arriving across the new land border with the EU in Ireland. Totally free of the jurisdiction of the European Court of Justice? The government now admits there will be continued 'indirect' subservience to European judges after all.[28] The list of fabrications, half-truths, exaggerations and downright lies that were deployed by the leaders of the Brexit campaign goes on.

There's a fairly simple rule in politics: if you make a promise and then fail to deliver it, you should be held to account. It's a rule that I know better than most. I was punished at the ballot box in part because I led a party that was unable to deliver one specific policy, during half a decade in government: even though we hadn't won the previous election, I wasn't Prime Minister, there wasn't enough money available, and we introduced numerous other progressive reforms and policies – still we got our knuckles badly rapped.

Millions of goods and services are bought and sold every day on a 'sale, return and refund' basis, in case they are found to be faulty or deficient.

Surely a principle that applies to the acquisition of a new fridge, or a pair of shoes, should apply to the way in which Brexit was sold falsely to millions of voters? There are many reasons to revisit the Brexit referendum outcome, but this is the most compelling of all: we took the decision on a false prospectus. Voters were sold a dodgy promise on a false basis. So they now have every right to withdraw their consent.

A year on from the referendum, the politicians with the loudest voices during the Leave campaign – Gove, Johnson, Davis, et al. – are sitting comfortably around the Cabinet table, taking home six-figure ministerial salaries and getting away with their fibs to the British people. Even Dominic Cummings, who took such pride in his cynical pledge on the NHS, now describes the referendum as a 'dumb idea' and accepts there is a chance that 'leaving will be an error'.[29]

Then there is the simple cost – to you and every family across the country – of Brexit. Far from being a sunny upland of milk and honey, Brexit Britain is turning out to be an increasingly expensive place. The economic storm clouds just keep on gathering; as it happens, the price of milk[30] and honey[31] are predicted to rise partly as a consequence of Britain's decision to quit the EU.

Following the vote to leave the European Union, there is no denying the stark reality: Brexit spells uncertainty for businesses and families the length and breadth of the UK. The economic benefits to a nation supposedly 'liberated from the shackles of Brussels' are nowhere to be seen. Just over a year after the Brexit referendum, it turns out that the eurozone is growing twice as fast as the British economy. So much for economic liberation.

While the full extent of the economic damage that Brexit is already inflicting on the British people would require a book of its own, it is easy to summarise: every chart, graph or measure tells the same grim story. The vote for Brexit is having a widespread and negative effect on the economy. These are not predictions, nor can they be dismissed as the findings from the experts that Michael Gove was so quick to denigrate. Economic uncertainty is taking its toll. It is not Project Fear. It is Project Reality.

The pound, for so long a symbol of pride for champions of Brexit, has suffered one of the largest devaluations in its history. Following steady losses in the months running up to the referendum, the pound saw the biggest one-day fall on record – worse than that caused by the shockwaves from the collapse of Lehman Brothers in 2008, and worse than 'Black Wednesday' on 16th September 1992, when the UK tumbled out of the European Exchange Rate Mechanism.

A year after the vote, the pound is worth around 15 per cent less against the euro and the dollar. Compared with the summer of 2015, when the reality of the impending referendum set in and the decline in sterling began, it is around 20 per cent lower.[39] Let's be clear why that is: it's the judgement of the currency markets that the UK's growth potential is significantly less than it was before the referendum. And that uncertainty is made all the worse by the government's insistence that it will take Britain out of the Single Market, as well as by its foot-stamping threats to walk away from the negotiating table.

Compare the Brexit devaluation to the devaluation of sterling in 1967, when a 14.3 per cent fall was seen as a humiliating defeat for Harold Wilson's government. When Wilson said that 'the pound in your pocket' is still worth a pound, he was held up to ridicule, as it was flagrantly untrue.

And so it is now. As the pound devalues, imported goods cost more, so prices go up. You can buy less with each pound in your pocket. That is why the rate of inflation hit 2.7 per cent in May

2017,[33] having been close to zero for the previous eighteen months, and why it is predicted to rise further. Consumers are paying the price.

Check your energy bills. Look at the price of filling your car with petrol. Compare how much you ended up paying for your summer holiday to Europe, or the US, this year compared to last. See how much it costs to replenish your winter wardrobe. Brace yourselves for rising bills at the supermarket checkout. This is all happening now.[34] Looking further into the future, one academic study forecasts that the prices of imported foods are likely to rise by 22 per cent.[35] Everything is costing more, and the least well off will inevitably feel the most pain. It's enough to make you reach for a fortifying glass of wine – unfortunately, the average price of a bottle has, since Brexit, hit its highest price ever.[36]

In normal times, wage growth would compensate for rising prices. But these aren't normal times. The economy is still recovering from the cardiac arrest of the 2008 economic crash, and people are experiencing the longest pay squeeze in seventy years.[37] A rise in prices, with no corresponding rise in wages, simply means that millions of Britons are poorer. Our standard of living will be lower. Just as things were beginning to look as if they might have started to get better, after many years of austerity – wages were finally starting to outpace prices in 2016[38] – Brexit is steamrollering the recovery backwards again.

This isn't simply about the price of things on supermarket shelves. It's also about the raw materials on which our economy relies. When import costs go up, it has a knock-on effect on everything from food production to complex engineering. So the Brexit squeeze on sterling means the economy will grow less quickly. That's why GDP growth fell to 0.2 per cent in the first quarter of 2017. Remarkably, the UK had the slowest rate of growth of all the twenty-seven other countries of the EU. It went from being the fastest-growing economy in the G7 in 2016 to the joint slowest (with Italy) in the first three months of 2017.[39]

For businesses, this is only part of the story. Many firms – particularly farms and factories – are struggling with a shortage of labour, as EU workers stay away, either because of the impact of devaluation on their pay packets or because of a perception that the UK is no longer as open to foreigners as it used to be. For example, about 80,000 seasonal workers a year pick and process British fruit and veg, and most of them come from the EU. By the summer of 2017 the National Farmers Union was reporting that farms had 17 per cent fewer seasonal workers than they needed.[40]

Workers are nervously eyeing the foreign investors on whom so much of our economy – and their jobs – depends. Our foreign direct investment (FDI) stock represents around half (48 per cent) of our GDP, with our economy being more dependent on FDI than any other large economy. For comparison, Japan's figure is 4 per cent. A total of four million UK employees work for companies that benefit from FDI. Two million of these are with companies that received investment from the EU.[41]

So warning bells were ringing when it was announced that the car industry had suffered a sharp drop in investment, from £2.5bn in 2015 to just £322m in the first half of 2017.[42] Firms such as Nissan and Toyota, as well as private investors, have chosen the UK precisely because it provides access to a Single Market of 500 million consumers. As the Japanese government pointedly put it, in a memo to the British government in September 2016, their businesses were 'invited by the Government in some cases, have invested actively in the UK, which was seen to be a gateway to Europe, and have established value-chains across Europe'.[43] Once the UK ceases to participate fully in the Single Market, the rationale for that investment will diminish sharply.

In some cases it's already happening, with companies moving staff and operations to the continent, to be sure of being able to continue to operate there after March 2019:

- EasyJet's European HQ is relocating to Vienna.
- Nestlé Blue Riband production has shifted to Poland.
- Deutsche Bank, Standard Chartered, J.P. Morgan, Goldman Sachs and other banks have laid out plans to move thousands of jobs out of London, mainly to Frankfurt and Dublin.
- Money-transfer company Transferwise, one of the biggest fintech firms in Europe, said in early April 2017 that it will move its HQ to the continent.
- In February, a study from KPMG showed that one in three manufacturing firms plans to shift its operations outside the UK.[44]

That list will continue to grow, with other banks and insurance companies in particular planning to open new European operations outside the UK. Before we say 'good riddance' to departing financial-services companies, let's remember that

they contribute more than £70bn a year in tax –
or 11.5 per cent of all taxes collected by the
government.

So prices are going up. The cost of living is
increasing. Businesses and firms are plotting escape
routes from Brexit Britain. Sadly, this sorry story
then gets even worse, because public services will
inevitably become the next victim of the declining
confidence in Britain's economy. In November 2016
the Chancellor revealed a significant Brexit black
hole in public finances over the next five years –
brought about by lower growth, less trade and a
shrinking EU workforce. The money the Treasury
will have to borrow or raise from more taxes, to fill
that black hole, is money that will not go towards
cutting waiting times in A&E, keeping NHS beds
open or paying for vital medicines. It will not go
towards easing the intense pressure on local care
services for older people. It will not go towards
reversing the shameful cuts to school budgets.
Instead, it is money that will go towards filling a
new Brexit black hole of our own making.

In part, the general-election result of June 2017 was
a clear message from the electorate that it had grown
tired of the long years of austerity. Despite numerous
unanswered questions about Labour's uncosted

shopping list of promises, it is clear that many voters preferred Corbyn's more optimistic pitch to the Conservative programme of further cost-cutting. Sensing the shift in mood, leading Brexiteers like Boris Johnson and Michael Gove were quick to shed crocodile tears about the continuing restraints on public-sector wages. But the truth is that it is their determination to pull us out of the EU, and the consequences on inflation and prices, that have led to the new pressure on take-home pay.

Philip Hammond, the Chancellor, has admitted that nobody voted to leave the EU to make themselves poorer. Unfortunately, that is exactly what is happening. We face an agonisingly stark choice as a country: millions of voters have signalled that they want to soften or halt austerity; yet softening or halting austerity is simply impossible, if we go ahead with Brexit. Brexit makes us poorer as a country – and a poorer country has less scope to stop belt-tightening.

Of course there are undoubtedly some voters who backed Brexit, but were never taken in by the lies of the Brexiteers and have always accepted that there would be an economic cost. What really mattered to them, above all, was the prospect of recapturing sovereignty – of our institutions and traditions, of our courts and Parliament – which has been steadily diluted over four decades of cross-continental cooperation inside the EU. Clawing back that sovereignty, they would claim, must come at a price. For them, arguments about the lies from leading Brexiteers or the effects on the economy will have little impact.

But how would they feel if it now emerges that the claims about recapturing sovereignty were false, too? What if Brexit means that we end up losing – not gaining – control over our own affairs?

A vote on 23rd June 2016, the Brexiteers insisted, was a chance to fight back against meddlesome Brussels bureaucrats and their pesky rules, regulations and red tape. Do you want your bananas to be bendy? Do you want to be free of EU rules determining the noise level of your Hoover? Do you want to rid Britain of intrusive EU regulations setting the maximum power for hairdryers? Then vote Leave. These were all examples given by Boris Johnson, when he attacked the EU because it wanted to 'dictate to the British people' how we live our lives. He famously urged voters to make 23rd June Britain's 'independence day'. The leading Brexiteers painted a bright future in which we could draw on our triumphant past – back to a glorious era when the Royal Yacht ruled the waves, Britain was a global, swashbuckling power and bluebirds sang merrily over the white cliffs of Dover.

Yet, far from leading us towards a rebirth of British greatness and sovereignty, the evidence so far suggests that Brexit is instead leading us towards greater national enfeeblement. Far from being the patriotic thing to do, Brexit is weakening the greatness in Great Britain. Our past provides us with much to be proud of. But pride should not topple into a false sense of superiority. Pride in our past does not serve as a realistic road map for our future. Far from returning us to our heritage as a great and respected global power, Brexit risks making us an object of mockery and bewilderment around the world. Indeed, the world watches on with increasing bafflement at the soap opera of British politics. Where has that great British tradition of pragmatism, sangfroid and common sense gone? To many foreign observers, Shakespeare's 'precious stone in the silver sea' has lost its shine; the sceptred isle has lost its lustre.

Today, except for a handful of tiny outposts such as the Pitcairn Islands (population: forty-two), the globe is no longer dominated by a very British pink colour. Despite this incontestable truth, some of the loudest – and most deluded – critics of our involvement in the European Union still cleave to a vision of a powerful 'Anglosphere' of nations, with Britain at the heart of a post-colonial network stretching from America to Australia via the subcontinent. Bound together by a shared language and, mostly, by a love of cricket, the Anglosphere can, its proponents argue, bring back the best of empire and allow us to cut our ties with the EU. Not only does this outlook fail to grasp the basic rules of geography and the passing of time, but it also ignores the fact that we are uniquely placed to take advantage both of our proximity to continental Europe *and* of being at the heart of the Commonwealth. We don't need to choose.

There is an unavoidable truth for Britain, as it reflects on its role in the twenty-first century: we are now a medium-sized nation, and we have to work with others in order to play an influential role in the modern world. This doesn't mean a ceding of power. As a member of the European Union, we were pooling decision-making authority with other countries, so ensuring that our collective clout counted for more than that of a country on its own. Were we ceding power? Not at all. By pooling our sovereignty, we were extending our power and influence over the world around us. The whole is very much greater than the sum of its parts.

During the referendum campaign one Conservative politician, arguing that Britain should remain in the EU, explained the equation rather well. 'International, multilateral institutions … invite nation states to make a trade-off: To pool and therefore cede some sovereignty in a controlled way, to prevent a greater loss of sovereignty in an uncontrolled way, through for example military conflict or economic decline.'[45] Theresa May saw what was at stake clearly when she uttered these words in April 2016. She has sounded a lot less convincing ever since.

Terrorism, trade and climate change do not respect borders. We can't mount an effective response to Russia, Syria or North Korea on our own. A strong Britain is one that works together with our neighbours to meet these challenges, not one that retreats into backward-looking nostalgia. Pooling sovereignty gives us more control of our future; being part of a larger bloc gives us greater influence and a bigger say in shaping events across the globe.

Don't take my word for it. Just look at how the world's largest nations have reacted to Brexit. Since the referendum the leaders of two of the world's most significant new powers, Prime Minister Narendra Modi of India and President Xi Jinping of China, have visited Europe on more than one occasion. Both have been to Germany to hold talks with Angela Merkel. Modi has also been to Spain and France. Xi has taken trips to Belgium and the Netherlands. Neither has come to the UK since the Brexit referendum.

Both Xi and Modi know that it makes far more sense to do business with a major bloc rather than with an isolated nation. The UK was noticeably absent when China and the EU issued a joint statement on forging ahead with the Paris Accords on tackling climate change. Prime Minister Modi has talked about restarting the planned India–EU trade and investment agreement – an agreement held up by Home Office objections in Whitehall when Theresa May was Home Secretary. When President Trump ripped up the Trans-Pacific Partnership on trade, how did Japan respond to US isolationism? Not by turning to so-called 'Global Britain'. Instead, with barely a glance across the Channel, Japan signed one of the largest trade deals on the planet with the EU. Far from gaining control, we are losing it fast. The world is moving on without us.

It was Dean Acheson, the US Secretary of State under President Truman, who famously quipped in 1963 that 'Great Britain has lost an Empire and has not yet found a role.' But his prediction proved to be wrong. In the years since then, we *had* found a crucial role, blending our EU membership, our place on the UN Security Council, our status as Europe's leading defence and foreign-policy heavyweight and our unique relationship with Washington. Our stable institutions, our first-rate universities, our world-beating financial centre, our reliability in global affairs – these and so many other qualities allowed us to punch well above our weight.

Yet every single one of those qualities has now been thrown into doubt by Brexit. Dean Acheson's prediction has finally come into its own, more than fifty years late, because of Brexit. We are a country adrift – no longer taken as seriously by global powers as we were before, and thrashing around trying to make sense of our own Brexit contradictions. We look, to all intents and purposes, like a country that has suddenly lost its way.

And yet, even if some readers find these arguments persuasive, there might still be one major reason why they would nonetheless be tempted to vote for Brexit again: to put firmly in their place the sanctimonious, metropolitan, global elite who wanted Britain to remain in the EU.

The truth is that voting for Brexit felt so good to so many people because it felt like a victory of ordinary voters against the arrogance of an out-of-touch political elite. It was a triumph of the many against the elitist few. But what if this is also turning out to be untrue as well?

In a speech in Mississippi in support of Donald Trump's presidential campaign, Nigel Farage hailed the vote for Brexit as a victory for the 'little people, the real people ... the ordinary, decent people'. A few months later Mr Farage, a privately educated ex-City trader with a taste for a post-prandial glass of port, flew across the Atlantic to join President Trump at the billionaire's victory party. There is a famous photo of the pair celebrating in front of one of Trump Tower's gold-plated lift doors. The little people must have been just out of shot.

The image was comical, but that meeting of narrow minds was an insight into a far darker aspect of the Brexit vote. For when the champions of the Leave vote insist that the referendum result must for ever be venerated as the will of the people, what they don't tell you is that a small, mostly elderly, mostly male collection of party donors, media barons, obsessive newspaper editors and opportunist hedge-fund managers have been driving the Brexit agenda, it would appear largely for their own ends. The best way to describe them is, as it happens, as an elite. It's a highly influential elite, too. So as

Britain stumbles, remember this: all this was brought to you, *bought* for you, by the Brexit elite.

This is not an attempt to suggest that the Brexit eruption was not fuelled by grass-roots discontent. It was, of course – but the ideas, money and propaganda that turbocharged the campaign were provided by an unaccountable array of vested interests, none of whom could ever claim to be representatives of ordinary people. So what exactly was in it for them?

The nature of the Brexit elite takes some unpicking. From the moment they were first elected to Parliament, many Conservative MPs have defined their political careers through their obsessive loathing of the EU. While some names will sound familiar – the likes of John Redwood and Liam Fox, for example – many others have toiled away for their cause in relative obscurity. By means of Westminster dining clubs and an array of Conservative Party committees and groupings, these MPs plotted, planned and ensured that Euroscepticism pulsated through the Conservative Party bloodstream.[46] However, while they may believe that their influence is considerable, the truth is that they merely served as the worker bees in the Brexit revolution. Running behind and alongside those Eurosceptic parliamentary networks are a handful of campaign groups and think tanks.[47] Some of these outfits attempted to provide intellectual ballast to the Brexit case, while those bodies with a more campaigning edge have evolved over the years into the forms that we would recognise from the referendum campaign: the Vote Leave and Leave.EU campaigns.

Well, you might well ask, what is wrong with that? Is it not admirable to fight for a cause in which you believe? Look a little closer. Over the years, the same names just keep on coming up. Rarely straying from the shadows, a handful of multimillionaire businessmen have, in some cases for thirty years or more, bankrolled whichever party or politician or think tank or campaign group stands on the most aggressive EU-bashing platform. Time and again, this small cast list – amongst them Paul Sykes, Peter Cruddas, Stanley Kalms, Stuart Wheeler, Michael Hintze and Patrick Barbour – repeatedly emerge as major Eurosceptic donors and backers of either the Conservative Party or UKIP.

The City of London is largely portrayed as pro-EU, or at least pro-Single Market, but some very rich City men began to push game-changing sums towards the Leave side of the campaign.[48] Why were they so interested in securing a particular result? In part, it seems, for reasons of self-interest: these phenomenally wealthy men view the financial regulations of the EU as burdensome and want to see the UK reinventing itself as a low-tax/low-regulation economy that is no longer bound to work with our European allies and no longer beholden to a set of shared standards.

- Peter Hargreaves, a co-founder of stock-brokers Hargreaves-Lansdowne and one of Britain's richest men, donated £3.2m to Vote Leave. He has explained that he is pro-Brexit because 'we will be insecure again. And insecurity is fantastic.'[49]
- Stuart Wheeler, a man who made his fortune as a founder of a spread-betting firm, once donated £5m to the Conservative Party. He has since given around £500,000 to UKIP, before donating more than £600,000 to Vote Leave. So why does he hate the EU? Because of 'its interminable regulations and restrictions on what businesses can do'.[50]
- Peter Cruddas, the multimillionaire former Tory donor, gave around £350,000 to Vote Leave because 'the EU concentrates on regulation and restriction'.[51]
- Michael Farmer, another hedge-fund manager, is worth more than £2bn. A Tory

Party donor and peer, he donated £300,000
to Vote Leave after complaining about 'the
relentless encroachment of Brussels legislation on the City'.[52]

- Anthony Bamford, who secured a peerage
  and had made generous donations to the
  Conservative Party, made a donation
  through his company JCB of more than
  £700,000 to the Leave campaign because
  he wants 'a deal that will allow us to become
  a truly global trading nation'.[53]

- Multimillionaire asset manager Jeremy
  Hosking gave around £1.7m to fund the
  campaign to get Britain out of the EU,
  despite admitting that 'if we take back
  sovereignty, there might be some short-
  term economic pain'.[54]

- Robert Edmiston, the chairman of International Motors, donated around £800,000
  to Vote Leave and declared that he couldn't
  'understand surrendering sovereignty ... to
  people who we don't know and didn't elect
  and who we can't remove or replace'.[55]

- Between them, hedge-fund managers
  Michael Hintze – who has donated millions
  to the Conservative Party – and Crispin

    Odey gave more than £700,000 to the
    Leave campaign.

- The Brexit money-man least averse to
  seeking publicity is Arron Banks. He made
  his fortune through various insurance
  companies and gave considerable sums to
  UKIP, is reported to have donated around
  £7.5m to the Leave campaign and partici-
  pated in the Trump Tower celebrations.
  'I don't want to be part of some French–
  German coalition. Power should be with
  Parliament,' Banks complained during the
  referendum. This particular multimillionaire
  later declared that a loss in household
  incomes after Brexit 'was a price worth
  paying to get back our own democracy'.[56]

I doubt very much that many – maybe any – of
those names are familiar to you, and I doubt whether
their money alone could have bought the referendum result. The Brexit elite, however, wields
influence in many ways. A small group of newspaper
owners and editors – again, all men, none of them
young – have made it a lifetime's work to attack
the European Union. Their visceral loathing of the
EU has shaped their respective papers' tone and

coverage for decades; little wonder that in his 2013 report into the ethics of the British press, Lord Leveson concluded that there was 'clear evidence of misreporting of European issues'.[57]

Rupert Murdoch, the 86-year-old Australian-born owner of *The Sun*, Richard Desmond, the UKIP-financing owner of the *Express*, and the billionaire Barclay brothers, the owners of the *Telegraph* newspaper group, all have editors who fill their papers with anti-European rhetoric. Desmond once explained his motivation, saying: 'I don't know if we should be in [the EU] or not, but I don't like being controlled by Brussels and these faceless people.'[58] He apparently prefers control by unelected newspaper proprietors and hedge-fund managers instead.

Paul Dacre, the secretive multimillionaire editor of the *Daily Mail* for the last quarter of a century, also features prominently in this cabal of unelected older men. Dacre enjoys a £1.5m annual salary and leads a peculiarly sheltered existence, which is reported to take him, in a chauffeur-driven car, between his various residences – including a shooting estate in Scotland – and his editor's chair in a plush office in central London.[59] Despite this, he claims to stand up for 'ordinary people' in their – or is it his? – fight against the 'metropolitan classes'.[60] One wonders when Dacre meets ordinary people, but the Britain he claims to speak for is, if his paper's columns are to be believed, being destroyed by immigrants. His obsession with foreigners saw the *Mail* lead with immigration warnings – including parroting the Leave campaign's absurd warnings that if Britain remained in the EU, it would be overrun by Turkish immigrants – on seventeen of the twenty-three weekdays before the referendum.[61]

Sadly, the referendum result does not appear to have sated Dacre's appetite for vitriol. In 2016 Dacre's paper attacked three High Court judges as 'Enemies of the People', after the trio ruled that the government must secure Parliament's approval to formally begin the Brexit process, while Theresa May's decision to call a snap election was met with a slightly demented front-page headline to 'Crush the Saboteurs'. The democratic process, the judiciary and the views of the 48 per cent of people who did not vote to leave the EU are not, it seems, of any concern to some parts of the Brexit elite.

Perhaps most strikingly of all, the Brexit elite stretches well beyond Britain itself. Some of the key players neither live nor pay taxes in the UK. The Legatum Institute – a think tank driven by a libertarian, low-regulation philosophy and amateur ideas about Britain's future trade policy – has deep pockets linked to offshore finance, and is so well connected to the heart of Whitehall that it was invited, inexplicably, to join a cast of top corporate chief executives in a meeting with David Davis in his country residence, Chevening, in the summer of 2017.[62] Dizzyingly wealthy individuals in the US have lent their financial clout to support libertarian US think tanks, in their promotion of small government, low tax and in some cases environmentally questionable policies – an ideological outlook that overlaps with anti-EU thinking across Europe. Through articles and public platforms, such bodies[63] have played a part in supporting and promoting the likes of Nigel Farage, far-right French presidential candidate Marine Le Pen and her Dutch counterpart, Geert Wilders. Following Donald Trump's election as US President, this ideology now echoes strongly on both sides of the Atlantic.

When Trump became President, he employed Steve Bannon as his White House Chief Strategist (he has since departed). Bannon previously ran the alt-right media outlet Breitbart in Washington and helped to set up its London branch, where he appointed one Raheem Kassam (later a chief of staff to Farage, and briefly a candidate to succeed him as UKIP leader) to edit the site. 'We look at London and Texas as two fronts in our current cultural and political war,' declared Bannon,[64] who is also on record as declaring that 'strong nationalist movements in countries make strong neighbours'[65] and that people 'don't believe in this kind of pan-European Union'. It is hard to know how much Trump takes on board, but in an interview with *The Times* in January 2017 the US President declared that the EU is 'basically a vehicle for Germany ... That's why I thought the UK was so smart in getting out.'[66] The interview was conducted by leading Leave campaigner Michael Gove. It was later confirmed that Rupert Murdoch was present throughout.[67]

The Brexit elite share a vision for Britain. They want to create a low-tax, low-regulation nation, a Singapore on stilts that stands precariously on its own, cast adrift from Europe and, so they argue, able to do as it pleases. Or rather, in the case of this elite, able to do as *they* please. Far from helping the 'little people', Brexit is intended to lead to the empowerment of rich old men, at the expense of everyone else.

But while the Brexit elite played a decisive role in making Brexit happen, they cannot be held responsible for the conduct since the referendum of the Brexit talks themselves. For that display of serial incompetence, only government ministers and their advisers are responsible. It is their job to negotiate the best deal possible for the nation – and they are making a spectacular hash of it. So much so, indeed, that for many people who voted Brexit, the humiliating spectacle of our government constantly arguing with itself, rather than negotiating effectively with the EU, is starting to put them off the whole thing.

It all sounded so simple. Boris Johnson's vision of Brexit was a gluttonous one: pro-cake, and pro-eating it. That won't happen. Liam Fox, the International Trade Secretary, declared a few months after the referendum that the UK's trading arrangement with the European Union would be 'at least as free' after Brexit as it is now. What's more, he boasted, he would soon conclude a shopping list of new bilateral trade deals around the world. That isn't going to happen either. David Davis had promised that Britain would be part of a free-trade area 'almost twice the size of the EU' within two years of the Brexit vote – a statement outdone in its absurdity only by Mr Davis' later boast of negotiating a trading area 'probably ten times the size of the European Union'. Based on

GDP, Davis is aiming for something larger than the economies of the entire planet combined.[68] So it can't happen.

Over and over again we have seen that the gap between the government's rhetorical bravado and the realism of the negotiations is vast. David Davis, the country's Brexit negotiator, had promised the 'row of the summer', as he vowed he would ensure that Britain's post-Brexit trade talks ran in parallel with its divorce discussions. At his first meeting with Michel Barnier, the man leading the negotiations for the EU, Davis backed down. Before the summer, he also slipped out a statement which acknowledged that the 'UK has obligations to the EU ... that will survive the UK's withdrawal', an acceptance that, despite months of bluster, the UK has outstanding payments to the EU – as any departing member of a club would do, when settling its tab – that it will have to meet. It's becoming increasingly difficult to understand what Mr Davis had in mind when he swaggeringly insisted that he would secure a 'deal like no other in history'.

The Prime Minister's own performance has hardly inspired confidence, either. Before the election, when she should have been reaching out to our European allies, Theresa May instead issued faintly paranoid warnings of EU plots against

Britain. For months she refused to give assurances that EU nationals living in the UK could remain, as before, and bullishly threatened that the EU would have to pay its own Brexit bill for Britain to leave. It was a case of losing friends and influencing nobody. Given her weakened position, and the growing realisation across the EU that her government is woefully underprepared for the talks, any further attempt at brinkmanship will fail. Any further warnings of plots will convince the EU that our Prime Minister is losing her own.

Following her failure to secure a majority in the 2017 election, the Prime Minister no longer has the authority to control her ministers or, it seems, to unite a divided government. With nobody to rein them in, her ministers are merrily biting chunks out of each other. In a clear swipe at Boris Johnson, Chancellor Philip Hammond used a speech in Germany to explain how 'compromise is the art of dividing the cake'. Mr Hammond also made the case for an extended four-year transitional period after Britain leaves the EU. In response, David Davis accused his Cabinet colleague of making 'a false distinction' and of issuing statements that are 'not quite consistent with each other'. There has even been the truly surreal sight of two Cabinet ministers, Health Secretary Jeremy

Hunt and Business Secretary Greg Clark, writing a letter to the *Financial Times* to shift their own government's policy – arguing that our current relationship with the EU 'remains the best way to promote improved patient outcomes both in Europe and globally'.[69]

All of this begs an obvious question: how can the government successfully negotiate Brexit when it doesn't appear to have finished negotiating with itself? The EU's chief negotiator, Michel Barnier, well prepared and waiting patiently for the UK to engage in constructive talks, appears as baffled as anyone. 'I am not sure whether [these points] have been fully understood across the Channel,' he reflected, when explaining that the UK could not withdraw from the Single Market and Customs Union and expect to retain all the benefits.

He is not alone in wondering whether many around the Cabinet table have, even now, managed to get to grips with the huge complexities of Brexit. Following the election it was revealed that no government department had yet conducted an analysis of the impact of leaving the Single Market; while Sir Amyas Morse, the man who heads the UK's public-spending watchdog, has described the government's Brexit plan as 'vague'. A year after the referendum, and even after the government published a number of position papers concerning Brexit in the summer of 2017, the uncertainty just keeps growing. Was any real thought given to what Brexit would mean for the border between the Irish Republic and Northern Ireland? When the Prime Minister declared that she would pull Britain out of the remit of the European Court of Justice (ECJ), did she realise that the court is the ultimate arbiter for a myriad of crucial day-to-day activities, from mobile telephone roaming charges to cross-border police cooperation and the mutual recognition of professional qualifications? Without a deal, will our aeroplanes even be able to land at European airports? The airline industry has repeatedly warned that flights could be grounded, if the UK leaves the EU's Open Skies Agreement. What does Brexit mean for the nuclear industry? The government has admitted that it did no formal assessment into the consequences of leaving Euratom, the non-EU, Europe-wide nuclear agency that is vital for nuclear research and safety, but which happens to be subject to ECJ rulings. Ed Vaizey and Rachel Reeves, a Conservative and a Labour MP who have combined to campaign to keep the UK in Euratom, are absolutely right when they point out that 'whatever people were voting for last June, it certainly wasn't to junk 60 years of co-operation in this area with our friends and allies'.[70]

David Cameron was often derided as being the essay-crisis Prime Minister. But at least, in the end, most of the time he got the essay done. From what I can see, Theresa May's government has barely managed to put together a single coherent paragraph on what Brexit will mean in practice. To be fair, Whitehall has expended a fair amount of ink on the government's Brexit position papers, but they were widely (and rightly) condemned as posing more questions than they provide answers. In some instances – for example, the lack of any concrete detail on how to police the new UK/EU border in Ireland, or the assertion that the UK will leave the Customs Union with the EU, while still retaining all the benefits of it – there appears to have been no progress in government thinking at all.

On top of this lack of preparation, the government is attempting to steer an extremely complex piece of legislation called the EU Withdrawal Bill through the Houses of Parliament. Formerly labelled by Brexiteers as the Great Repeal Bill, the downgraded title of this legislation shows that it is nothing of the sort. Essentially an enormous photocopying exercise, it will see thousands of elements of EU law copied and pasted into UK law, in an effort to ensure a smooth departure from the EU. This is a complicated task and, not surprisingly, opposition parties have vowed to make the government's life as difficult as possible. The bill will be immensely time-consuming, and will drain so much energy in Parliament and Whitehall away from the government's day-job of providing the public with decent public services, a growing economy and a sensible foreign policy.

Whatever one's views on the EU, no one can be content with a government that appears to be so paralysed by the task of Brexit that it has, to all intents and purposes, given up governing Britain in almost every other respect. Given how much there is to do to make our society fairer, our schools better, our hospitals more efficient and our economy stronger, this amounts to an unforgivable dereliction of national duty.

Boris Johnson's approach to cakes is a good allegory for the government's wider incompetence on Brexit. Having promised to bake you a cake, the Foreign Secretary is like a dinner-party guest who arrives at your home empty-handed, breezily insisting that he can still rustle up a dessert in no time. He then takes over the kitchen and begins to throw its entire contents into every pot and pan he can find. It is, of course, a recipe for disaster. At the end, he bolts out of the front door into the night, having emptied out your cupboards and having created the largest pile of washing-up your home has ever seen. You are then left to clean up the mess.

It is now many months since Article 50, the mechanism that officially started the two-year clock on Brexit talks, was triggered. Theresa May's decision to call a general election meant that months of precious negotiating time were wasted and that little to no progress has been made. Throughout that period the EU's negotiating team prepared properly for the talks ahead, agreeing settled positions and establishing how to achieve its aims. Perhaps gripped by a growing panic, government ministers continue to boast about the glorious deal they will secure. Meanwhile, as Michel Barnier drily observed, there's the growing sound of the 'clock ticking'.

If the government's shortage of competence wasn't bad enough, something else is now in very short supply, too: time. As of the autumn of 2017, there is a maximum of a year left for the UK and the EU to cross every 't' and dot every 'i' in pursuit of a fully fledged new deal setting out the terms on which the UK will leave the EU and operate outside it. Several months are needed for any such deal to be signed off by the EU's institutions, including the European Parliament, and then to be ratified by twenty-seven parliaments and some regional parliaments, too.

Even without Mrs May's shredded authority, her bickering ministers, the months wasted on electioneering and the sheer complexity of the task at hand, negotiating Brexit in a full two years would have been the biggest challenge this nation has faced since the Second World War. In my opinion, it is now simply impossible for a full deal – or even a complex interim deal – to be negotiated in what little time remains.

I can see only three possible outcomes.

The first is to continue in the direction we are currently limping towards: total failure. Unless the government fundamentally changes its approach to Brexit, the talks are likely to collapse and the UK will leave the EU without a deal. The impact of such a disorderly Brexit on the economy, on consumer prices and on public services would be severe. In the words of Chancellor Philip Hammond, no deal would be 'very, very bad for Britain'.

The second option is for the UK to secure an extension to the negotiating timetable. Article 50 contains a provision to extend negotiations if all member states agree. Alternatively, in the jargon of Brussels, the negotiators could simply 'stop the clock' – that is, suspend the talks for a certain period of time. The government would be wise to start exploring this route at once, but there are no indications that it is planning to ask for extra time, or a pause, and there is no guarantee that it would be granted, if it was requested.

Third, the government could accept that its economic and political interests are to remain within the Single Market and/or the Customs Union, either on a transitional basis (as now advocated by Labour) or permanently. One way or another, the UK would end up in a position similar to countries like Norway and Switzerland, outside the EU, but with access to its markets. While this option would do much to alleviate the negative impact of Brexit on the economy, and is certainly more desirable than leaving altogether, it would leave Britain in the unenviable position of abiding by the rules and regulations of the Single Market and the Customs Union while losing any chance to draft or veto them. We would, in effect, become rule-takers, not rule-makers. So much for taking back control. Brexiteers would not be alone in wondering if the whole sorry experience would have been worth it.

Knowing what we know today, can anyone honestly argue that Britain is set on the best course for its future? On any measure, scale or analysis, the answer is clear. In the short time since the referendum, the country has declined at a pace that even the gloomiest of Remain voters could never have predicted. The Prime Minister is not a politician famed for her flexibility or imagination, but as opinion shifts, she should be forced to reconsider her interpretation of the referendum result.

In June 2016, 16.1 million people – a larger number than have ever voted for a winning party in a general election – voted against Brexit. By choosing the hardest of Brexits, by attacking them as 'citizens of nowhere', Theresa May made the extraordinary choice to de-legitimise and ignore the millions of people who voted for a different future. She made no effort to reach out to them. She made no effort to include them in her pursuit of a post-Brexit settlement. She acted in a way that was small and divisive, when she had the opportunity to act big and be generous.

For one particular group of voters, the referendum result – and Mrs May's monochrome interpretation of it – was particularly cruel. In June 2016 more than 70 per cent of voters aged 18–24 voted for Britain to remain in the European Union, as did 62 per cent of 25–34-year-olds and 52 per cent of 35–44-year-olds.[71] Had 16- and 17-year-olds been allowed to vote in the referendum, their support for remaining in the EU would, according to one poll, have been overwhelming, with 82 per cent saying they would have voted for Remain.[72] Even in strongly Leave-supporting areas such as Lincolnshire, academic research has found that up to 90 per cent of schoolchildren backed remaining in the EU,[73] with their overwhelming cause of concern being the loss of the ability to live and work on the continent. Young people from across the country voted for (or would vote for, if they had the chance) a different future from the one now being imposed upon them.

The numbers tell a clear story: where Britain finds itself today, and the destination towards which it is stumbling, is not the one that the young of this country chose. And yet it is the one they will be forced to inhabit. This is an unforgivable act of generational theft, a deliberate rejection of the wishes of the very people who will be most affected by Brexit. There is no example anywhere else in the world of a mature democracy taking such an abrupt and radical decision about its own future, against the explicit and stated wishes of those who have to inhabit that future: the young.

Sadly, they are likely to be let down all over again. Turnout amongst 18–24-year-olds soared in the election on 8th June 2017 to its highest point in a quarter of a century, with more than 60 per cent of that age bracket casting their vote for Jeremy Corbyn's Labour Party.[74] It isn't hard to see why. Tired of Conservative austerity (which has been pursued since the election of 2015 in a far more regressive manner than the approach adopted by the Coalition government) and alarmed by Theresa May's pitch for a hard Brexit, they sought a change of direction for this country and liked what they saw in Mr Corbyn. Serving up a buffet of something-for-everyone where no one pays the bill, Labour's manifesto caught the imagination and, it seemed, everyone agreed with Jeremy Corbyn. In the run-up to the 2010 election I briefly experienced being the political flavour of the month. It's a good feeling. I'm sure Corbyn is enjoying his moment. But, as I know all too well, that moment won't last for ever. The rallies that took place across the country; the social-media frenzy; the sight of more than 150,000 people chanting the Labour leader's name while he shuffled across the Pyramid Stage at

Glastonbury – people, young people especially, believe that he can bring about the change they desperately want to see in this country.

Young people, Mr Corbyn told the packed field at Worthy Farm, voted for him because they were 'fed up with being denigrated, fed up with being told they don't matter'. He's right. But if any of those young people voted for the Labour Party because they believed it offered a different way forward for Britain's long-term relationship with Europe, they would soon discover how wrong they were. Within days of the election result John McDonnell, the Shadow Chancellor, confirmed his view that 'people will interpret membership of the Single Market as not respecting that referendum'. A month before the general election the Labour leader had insisted that Brexit was 'settled'. So much for standing up for those who feel they don't matter. This lifelong Eurosceptic sailed through the election campaign whilst barely uttering a word on Brexit. Now, riding high in the polls, facing a weakened government and with the parliamentary numbers to defeat it, Corbyn still chooses to say very little, leaving the announce-ment of his party's new approach to a Brexit transition period to Keir Starmer, Labour's spokes-person on Brexit. Yet he has the chance to speak up for the young, so many of whom voted for him because they believed he would give them back their European future.

Recent polling shows that eight out of ten Labour Party members support keeping Britain in the Single Market and the Customs Union – not temporarily, as espoused by the party, but permanently – while more than half would back a referendum on the final deal.[75] Crucially, the issue that perhaps animates the supporters of Jeremy Corbyn the most – austerity – is inextricably linked to Brexit. Corbyn refuses to come clean about the crippling contradiction in his own approach: he can try to end austerity by ending Brexit too, but he hasn't the slightest chance of ending austerity if he refuses to challenge Brexit. Labour's support for a 'soft' Brexit transition, in which Britain temporarily remains inside both the Single Market and the Customs Union, is of little consequence if it is merely succeeded by a hard Brexit. The outcome, from the point of view of Corbyn's many young supporters, will be the same: a hard Brexit, if on a slightly delayed timetable and, with it, the lengthened pain of austerity that it will inevitably bring. Everything, in fact, that these young, hopeful Labour supporters thought they were voting against.

If the political classes feel they can ignore the will of the young, they may find it harder to ignore a wider change in public sentiment. Politicians know it is a bad idea. Pundits can see it is a bad idea. Now, crucially, people are starting to feel it, too. At the start of the summer of 2017 there were some signs that public opinion was beginning to shift, not just against Theresa May's interpretation of Brexit, but against Brexit altogether. One polling company, Survation, showed that 54 per cent of people would now vote for Britain to remain in the European Union, should the referendum be held again.[76] Another, by the same company, revealed that 69 per cent of those polled now disagree with the Prime Minister's 'hard Brexit' stance, with only 35 per cent accepting her argument that no deal is better than a bad deal for Britain. In late August 2017 a poll by Opinium showed that if another referendum were held, Remain would win by 47 to 44 per cent;[77] a YouGov poll in the previous month had Remain winning by 46 to 43 per cent.[78]

The mantra of the Brexiteers is that the will of the people cannot be ignored. But the will of the people can change. Once the will of the people turns, and young and old join forces in their opposition to Brexit, then anything is possible.

So the prospects for Brexit Britain are not looking pretty. The economy is in serious trouble once again. Britain's standing in the world is diminishing. And the promises of Brexit have been broken. Those responsible for negotiating a good Brexit deal are conducting themselves with chaotic incompetence. As a nation, we appear to be in the grip of a spell, punching ourselves in the face over and over again, and yet somehow telling ourselves that there's nothing we can do about it. Do we really need to keep on with this baffling display of self-harm? If you saw someone in the street throwing right hooks at their own nose and upper cuts at their own chin, you would think they were in desperate need of help. If they stopped to listen, you would plead with them at least to pause for breath, before they knocked themselves out altogether. Ideally you would persuade them to walk away from a fight in which they would always be the loser. And Brexit, quite clearly, is a fight that will only do Britain harm.

Can the body-blows of Brexit be stopped before things get even worse? Of course they can. We remain at liberty to change course. Our destiny is in our own hands. We are not on a non-stop conveyor belt towards Brexit. As a nation, we have taken a decision to leave the EU, which is proving to be more costly, less beneficial and much more complex than we were told. So we are perfectly entitled to change our minds – and pursue a different course that can lead Britain back into the European fold.

How you can stop Brexit

As THEY BOWED DOWN before a seemingly invincible Theresa May when she succeeded David Cameron as Prime Minister, Conservative MPs – including those who had campaigned to keep Britain in the European Union – swore an oath of allegiance. 'We are all Brexiteers now,' they chanted.

We aren't, though, are we? For millions of people across the country, such a Damascene conversion did not take place on the morning after the referendum. In fact for millions of voters, especially as they see the facts accumulate against Brexit, the opposite is happening.

This book has sought to explain why it is right for the country to change its decision to leave the European Union, and why developments in Europe make it easier to do so than is widely believed. So as you walk the high streets of Britain, enjoy a pint in your local pub or take your daily commute to work, listen in to conversations and ask people what they are thinking. You will find that they are not, by any measure, all Brexiteers now. The words you are far more likely to hear today, whispered at first, but growing ever louder, go something like this: 'Brexit is turning out to be much harder than they said it would be. Maybe it wasn't such a good idea after all.' The mood is turning.

You can also hear the Brexiteers getting jittery. 'All these excitable people going on the TV better wake up to the fact that [Brexit] has to be delivered,' Conservative MP and leading Brexiteer Owen Paterson has complained. 'If it's not delivered, there will be the most terrible damage to the integrity of the political establishment.'[79] There you have it: the voice of the new Brexit elite worrying about the impact on the political establishment. Surely he, and everyone else, should be more worried about the damage being done to our country than to the reputation of the establishment?

It's time to set aside our peculiar combination of British fatalism and pride – this fear that nothing can be done about it now, the ship has sailed, and publicly admitting we were wrong would be a mistake. Surely there is no greater mistake than ploughing ahead with a course of action that makes less and less sense by the day?

So what happens next? Who can change the course of Brexit? *You* can. By deploying pressure, argument and passion, you can change the direction of our country. But to do so, you first need to change the approach taken by an all-important group of people: MPs. Theresa May has promised MPs a vote on the deal, once talks have concluded in October 2018. As I shall explain in more detail below, Parliament therefore has the power to halt the government's approach to Brexit. They could halt Brexit and then, if EU leaders were willing to continue talking, Britain could return to the nego-tiating table. So everything that follows in this chapter assumes that this is our target: getting MPs to vote down the deal they are presented with.

Although being an MP for twelve years – and Deputy Prime Minister for five – was undoubtedly the greatest privilege of my working life, I can't pretend I ever liked the House of Commons much. Notwithstanding all the colourful pomp and cere-mony, regardless of the yah-boo drama of Prime Minister's Questions, our Parliament is fundamen-tally dysfunctional and outdated, a Hogwartsian institution that, most of the time, is toothless to stop the government of the day doing what it likes.

Yet, right now, Parliament is still the key to stopping Brexit – because everything changed on 8th June 2017. Much to its own surprise, Parliament suddenly found itself with real, rather than mere theatrical, power over the future of our country.

Theresa May triggered a surprise election to seek a mandate for her extreme Brexit, urging the electorate to remember that 'every vote for the Conservatives will make me stronger'. It turned out that many voters did not want to make her stronger at all, or help her drive through her version of Brexit. Instead, the Prime Minister saw her majority shredded. Mrs May now leads a bickering government that owes its threadbare hold on power to Northern Ireland's Democratic Unionist Party. A controversial billion-pound deal has secured the votes of the DUP's ten Members of Parliament, giving the Prime Minister a working majority of just thirteen. It is an inauspicious number and it may not be enough. Remember, John Major's Conservative government began the 1992 Parliament with a majority of twenty-one. By 16th January 1997 it had been entirely whittled away.

So the government is vulnerable – increasingly a victim, not an author, of events – which puts the opposition in an unusually strong position to steer events. Indeed, the one person who could change the fate of this country more rapidly than anyone else is Jeremy Corbyn, the leader of the Labour Party. He could change the direction of this country in a heartbeat. If the Labour leader ordered every one of his MPs to reject the government's negotiated deal, then – with the support of Liberal Democrats, the SNP, the sole Green MP, Plaid Cymru and a very small number of Conservative rebels – that vote would be won.

If he went further and argued that the British people deserved another chance to vote on its European future, then he has the political strength, in view of the government's own weakness, to make it happen. When it comes to Brexit, Corbyn is the most important person in British politics today.

So far, the signs are not encouraging that he has either the will or the wish to intervene. Jeremy Corbyn has been a lifelong Eurosceptic. In the 1975 referendum he voted to leave the Common Market. In 1986 he voted against the Single Market. He opposed the Maastricht Treaty in 1992, voted against the Lisbon Treaty in 2007, and in 2016 he sleepwalked his way through the referendum. Mr Corbyn's efforts to campaign for Britain to remain in Europe were dismissed as 'risible' by Alan Johnson, the man who led Labour's campaign, in contrast to the Labour leader's full-throttle perform-ance in the subsequent general election.

Millions of voters, especially younger voters, flocked to Jeremy Corbyn at the general election because of a vague feeling that he had the right instincts on Brexit, and on ending austerity. Above all, they felt he staunchly opposed what the Conservatives stand for. Little did they realise that, on the most important issue of our generation – Brexit – he has walked hand-in-hand with Conservative Eurosceptics alongside whom he has been voting against Europe for decades.

During the general-election campaign in 2017 the bone-headed attack dogs in the right-wing press got it wrong, once again – by heaping abuse on Corbyn, they only made him more popular and dignified, in the eyes of his voters. Their vitriol allowed him to sail through the election without having to answer any meaningful questions on his policies, especially on Brexit. Seen by his supporters as possessing the wisdom of a monk, Mr Corbyn took a Trappist vow of silence on Brexit – and got away with it.

Emboldened by the election result and with his leadership of the party secure, Corbyn soon left no one in any doubt about his Euroscepticism. He sacked three of his frontbenchers for voting against the party in support of a Queen's Speech amendment that called for Britain to remain within the Single Market and the Customs Union. He even won the backing, at the time, of none other than Nigel Farage.[80]

And yet there is still every chance that Corbyn can be cajoled and pushed into a braver approach. For a start, his Shadow Cabinet remains deeply divided over the party's Brexit position, and many of them drop hints that if public opinion moves, then Labour could move with it. London Mayor Sadiq Khan, perhaps the second-most-influential Labour politician in Britain today, has made clear that Labour could promise to hold a second referendum on EU membership, if the mood suggests the public wants one.

Keir Starmer, the party's Brexit spokesperson, persuaded Jeremy Corbyn over the summer of 2017 to part company with the Conservatives on the content of a transition arrangement. By advocating a continuation of the status quo for a transitional period (unlike the Conservatives' increasingly implausible claim that the UK will leave the EU's Single Market and Customs Union in the spring of 2019), Corbyn and Starmer are merely acknowledging a practical reality – that there isn't time to negotiate anything more complex – whilst also making life as uncomfortable for the government as possible. But, if for no more than tactical reasons, this does at least suggest that Corbyn can be roused from his stupor of indifference towards Brexit, if there is sufficient political incentive for him to do so.

In other words, whilst there is no prospect under Corbyn of the Labour Party trying to *lead* public opinion away from Brexit, it may well choose to *follow* public opinion as it parts company with Brexit.

Which is where you come in. You can apply pressure on the Labour Party to rediscover its lost backbone when it comes to Brexit.

But, you might argue, Article 50 has been triggered. Does this not mean that Brexit, in whatever form it takes, is now inevitable? Hasn't the ship sailed? Isn't it too late to press the pause button? Actually, we don't know that for certain. Lord Kerr, the Scottish lawyer who authored Article 50, has himself said it 'is not irrevocable'. In the end, in the EU everything is political. European law has a habit of giving way where there is political will from the member states. If the UK changed its mind about Brexit, it would be open to us to ask the other twenty-seven members to stop the clock. There would no doubt be a diplomatic price to pay, but it could be done.

There's another alternative, too. Some eminent lawyers think Article 50 can be reversed unilaterally by the UK, without having to ask other countries' permission. This is likely to end up being tested in the courts. Assuming that interpretation is right, then all it would take to stop Brexit in its tracks would be a letter from the government, on the back of a vote in Parliament.

In all of this, I want you to look for inspiration from the most surprising quarter – from the very people who campaigned to drag Britain *out* of the European Union. Yes, Nigel Farage should be your role model. Not for his views, obviously, or for his divisive rhetoric, but for his sheer bloody-minded refusal to give up. And he wasn't alone. The battalion of greying Conservative MPs you have never heard of; the shady financiers of the Brexit elite; the loopy rantings of Paul Dacre; those obscure campaign groups and the obsessive scribblers of angry letters – all these people fought relentlessly for Brexit, over many years, long before the term 'Brexit' had even been invented. They were often subject to ridicule and frequently occupied the outer fringes of mainstream politics, but if they hadn't endlessly chipped away, then the political avalanche of the referendum would never have happened. At times it must have seemed as if nobody was listening. At times nobody *was* listening. In the end, however, they got their way.

'Those intent on trying to thwart the process, hoping something will magically appear, they are dreaming,' warned International Trade Secretary and arch-Brexiteer Liam Fox, as the voices against Brexit began to be heard. For more than a quarter of a century, from the moment he joined the ranks of Tory MPs rebelling against the Maastricht Treaty in 1992, Dr Fox wouldn't give up on his dream. So why should we?

Remember, too, the numbers involved. While 52 per cent of people who voted in the referendum ticked the box to leave the EU, that number represents only 37 per cent of the total voting population of Britain. Legally speaking, the referendum was an 'advisory' plebiscite only. To look at the result another way, the votes of just 650,000 people determined the outcome of the referendum. If we voted again tomorrow, the demographics of this country would have already shifted in favour of staying in the EU. The oldest voters – who supported Brexit in huge numbers – are, by their inescapable mortality, a declining proportion of the total number of voters, whilst younger voters – who overwhelmingly supported Remain – are becoming more active. In the month that followed Theresa May's calling of a snap election, 1.2 million British people aged between eighteen and thirty-five registered to vote, with about half being aged twenty-four or younger. Based on the last referendum, that's more than 650,000 Remain voters already. The tiny Brexit majority of the referendum may already have passed its highest peak.

So we are dealing with the narrowest and slimmest of margins. Every voice, every letter and every demonstration to reverse Brexit counts. The Members of Parliament whom *you* elected on 8th June 2017 have the power to change your future. They are there to serve you. They are there to listen to the will of the people.

But how, you may ask, is it possible to influence a political party? How can you make your views known to Jeremy Corbyn? Here's how: join the Labour Party and make your voice heard. It may seem odd for a former leader of the Liberal Democrats – and someone who has fought against the illiberal habits of Labour all my political life – to advocate joining the Labour Party. And, as a lifelong card-carrying member of another party, I won't be doing so myself. But if you are someone who has never joined a party, or perhaps has been inclined to join Labour but has never got round to it, or if you are simply someone who recognises that the importance of Brexit is far greater than individual party political allegiances, then I would urge you to take the plunge.

Once you have taken that step, try following this checklist of actions to make your opinions heard:

i)   **VISIT YOUR MP ONCE A MONTH**
ii)   **ATTEND LOCAL PARTY MEETINGS**
iii) **ATTEND PARTY CONFERENCE, AND TABLE MOTIONS**
iv)   **WRITE TO JEREMY CORBYN**
v)   **IF NECESSARY, WALK AWAY**

First, make sure *your* MP knows what *you* think about Labour's endorsement of the Tories' overall position on Brexit (notwithstanding differences about the transition). Labour MPs, by and large, believe Britain should be part of the EU – just ten of them are understood to have voted for Brexit – but many also feel that the will of the people has spoken and it cannot speak again. As we know, it can. So let them know by writing them emails and letters and, most importantly of all, by visiting them in person at one of their weekly advice surgeries once a month. As I know from my own experience as a constituency MP, there are few things that have as great an impact as people forcefully explaining themselves, in person. So do it, monthly, until they get the point.

Second, start attending local party meetings. As the Labour Party's official website makes clear, 'we welcome people to join the party from all walks of life, have their say and influence policy'. Pro-European Labour MPs need your support at local branch and Constituency Labour Party (CLP) meetings, with many currently under attack from party activists for their perceived disloyalty to Corbyn over Brexit. The last thing Labour needs is the election of more MPs so loyal to Corbyn that they won't challenge his Brexit views.

Third, submit policy proposals, learn how to table motions and then attend conference. Why not draft a motion and take it to your local branch meeting? If you can win support for it and get it passed, it will then be voted on by your CLP. Any motions passed by CLPs are sent to the relevant Shadow Secretary of State and the General Secretary of the party. You can also contribute to the National Policy Forum, at www.policyforum. labour.org.uk. This is the party's official policy-making process, and (in theory at least) all submissions on Brexit will be seen by the members of the International Policy Commission, which includes the Shadow Brexit Secretary and Shadow

Foreign Secretary. Throughout his tenure as Labour leader, Jeremy Corbyn has repeatedly stated that it is the membership that should shape party policy at conference – so start doing it. A one-day pass costs £29, access to the conference hall is £51. Learn the mechanisms and start pushing for policy change.

Fourth, keep reminding Jeremy Corbyn why you voted for him. If Labour members and voters were all to put pen to paper and write to the Labour leader with their concerns about Brexit, then Corbyn could hardly complain. After all, when he was elected as Labour leader his promise was to 'listen to everyone', because 'leadership is about listening'. So get writing. There's a template for you to follow in Appendix A at the end of the book.

Fifth, and finally, walk away if Labour doesn't listen to you. Jeremy Corbyn is proud of the increase in membership under his leadership. He's promised to 'mobilise this astonishing new force in politics, and ensure people in Britain have a real political alternative'. If he doesn't listen, and if he refuses to deliver the real alternative you want, then tear up your membership card. Don't let him take your support for granted.

Of course there are other parties to support and join. The Lib Dems, SNP, Plaid Cymru and the

Greens have a long-standing commitment to Britain's place in Europe. The Lib Dems, especially, have a particularly distinguished pro-European pedigree. It was one of the main catalysts that led to Roy Jenkins, Shirley Williams, Bill Rodgers and David Owen creating the breakaway Social Democratic Party, which later became part of the Liberal Democrats. For half a decade in Coalition government with the Conservatives from 2010 to 2015, the Lib Dems prevented the Conservative Party's Europhobic demons from engulfing the country. And once the Conservatives got their way in power on their own and triggered the Brexit referendum, the Lib Dems have been consistent in arguing for a way back into Europe.

But at a time of national emergency, and for as long as Parliament is dominated by Labour and Conservative MPs, it is undoubtedly true that what happens within the two larger establishment parties is of the greatest importance.

So if you can't stomach joining the Labour Party, if you are ideologically inclined in a Conservative direction in any event and if you also believe that Brexit is *the* issue of our times, then joining the Conservatives is another route to make your views felt. It may, at first, feel like entering the lion's den – the Conservative Party has mutated into a close imitation of UKIP in recent years. Its vicious internal divisions about Europe are not for the faint-hearted. But it's worth remembering that 176 of the 317 Conservative MPs are assumed to have voted for Remain; and, of the thirty-two new Tory MPs elected at the last election, there are eighteen who have declared that they voted to keep Britain in the EU.[81] They are *not* all Brexiteers now, and many are following neither their heads nor their hearts as they dutifully line up behind the Prime Minister. 'If we cancel Brexit we destroy ourselves, if we go ahead we destroy the country,' one minister was recently quoted as saying.[82] If the membership of the Conservative Party were to be swelled with new pro-European party members, then perhaps Conservative MPs would finally feel more emboldened to save the country.

Here is a handy checklist of steps you can take to drum some sense into the Conservatives:

i)   **JOIN THE PARTY**
ii) **CHALLENGE BREXIT MPs IN REMAIN SEATS**
iii) **VOTE IN THE LEADERSHIP CONTEST**
iv) **GO TO CONSERVATIVE PARTY CONFERENCE**
v)   **WRITE TO THERESA MAY**

First, sign up. A membership card costs £25 –
or just a fiver if you are under twenty-three. Here's
the link: https://www.conservatives.com/join.
A tiny proportion of the country makes up the
members of the Conservative Party – not much
more than 150,000 people. More than half of that
number are over sixty,[83] while a recent poll of party
members showed that 78 per cent wanted a hard
form of Brexit.[84] These are the people that Conservative MPs hear from, and they are the people they
must answer to. Make sure they hear another view.
Make sure they hear *your* view. If just 1 in 100
Remain voters were to join the Conservative Party,
they would outnumber the current membership of
the party.

Second, after becoming a member, you should
seek to join moves to challenge an MP who is
pushing for a hard Brexit, despite the majority of
his or her constituents disagreeing. Some of the
loudest advocates of an extreme Brexit hold
constituencies that voted to Remain in the EU:
Liam Fox, Iain Duncan Smith, John Redwood,
Chris Grayling, even Theresa May. They like to
bang on about the will of the people, but it turns
out they're happy to ignore it in their own back
yard. Perhaps it's time to make sure they listen.
A special general meeting of the local Conservative
association can be organised if a petition is signed

by more than fifty members, or 10 per cent of the total membership. The petition is then sent to the secretary of the executive of the association, requesting him or her to convene the meeting where a vote is held. Make these people know that they don't speak for you.

Third, use your membership to vote in any future Conservative Party leadership contest. The runners and riders make for grim reading. The most recent survey of party members has the neo-Edwardian figure of Jacob Rees-Mogg as their preferred choice to be the next leader of the party. Yes, really. Next in line are Brexit secretary David Davis and Foreign Secretary and leading Brexit campaigner Boris Johnson.[85] So sign up. Pressure your Conservative MP to support a pro-Remain candidate to make the run-off in any future leadership contest. And vote for them when you have the chance.

Fourth, sign up to attend the annual party conference. There's no obligation to purchase a 'Little Iron Lady Babygro' or a pair of Theresa May cufflinks, or the other political paraphernalia available at the conference shops. Just get there and make your voice heard. Don't cheer when a Conservative leader attacks the 'citizens of nowhere' or pesky 'human-rights lawyers'. Speak up in fringe meetings. Repeatedly push ministers on the government's policy and question their reasons for making Brexit so hard. The political media will be watching.

Fifth, and finally, write a letter to the Prime Minister. Should the message on each letter be the same, then the message will get through. Theresa May prides herself on her attention to detail and her capacity for hard work. She will read a sample of the letters that are addressed to her. So write to her, right now, to explain why she is wrong about Brexit. There's a template in Appendix B at the end of the book.

Of course, many political commentators and members of the Westminster village will dismiss this call for people to join the Labour and Conservative parties as a gimmick. Political party membership is not for the masses – only for those who are most enthusiastic or expert about politics – and mass infiltration by anti-Brexit voters is just silly mischief-making: that is what they'll say.

But what about the hundreds of thousands – probably millions – of Conservative voters who are uncomfortable about the direction this government is taking? Do they not have a right, as Conservative-inclined voters, to make their views known? And what about the many millions of Labour voters who are passionately in favour of our continued membership of the EU? Are they not allowed space in Jeremy Corbyn's party?

The truth is that, even with the recent increase in Labour and Lib Dem party membership, becoming a member of a political party is something that only a tiny fraction of the voting public does. And that's the whole problem: too much of our politics is dominated by what are, in effect, ideological sects, unrepresentative of wider society. Why should their narrow prejudices (in the case of the Conservative Party) or their personality cult (in the case of Corbyn's Labour Party) be the driving force of what shapes the future of our country? We *all* have a right to have our say, as the circumstances surrounding Brexit change and the promises that were made fail to materialise.

That is why I am suggesting you do something that has never happened before in modern politics. Don't leave this to the political parties to fix in a way that suits them. Force them to fix this agonising dilemma we face as a country to suit *you*. And the best way to make sure they will do that is to join them, even temporarily, and force the parties to change their ways. It is an ambitious proposal, but one that is deadly serious in intent. The future of our country depends on it.

Needless to say, many of you who are fired up by the issue of Brexit will still baulk at the idea of joining a political party to try and change it from within, especially if you're working on your own. It's the kind of thing best done in groups – strength and courage come in numbers. But even if you refrain from entering into party political waters, there are still things you can do to make your views known, and to spread the word that Brexit is not an inescapable fate.

Here is a checklist of five things you can do, outside of party politics:

i)   **PERSUADE FIVE FRIENDS AND NEIGHBOURS**
ii)   **JOIN A CAMPAIGN GROUP AND USE SOCIAL MEDIA**
iii)   **MOBILISE WITH OTHER VOLUNTEERS**
iv)   **MOBILISE YOUR UNION**
v)   **DEMONSTRATE!**

First, set out each month to persuade five friends, neighbours, family members or colleagues that Brexit can be halted and changed. Be relentless. Repeat the arguments made in this book. Above all, persuade those who have doubts about Brexit, but think it's too late to stop it, that they have every right to change their minds. We're not on a one-way conveyor belt to economic decline. We can get off it and start again. Persuade them, and then persuade them to persuade others. Before you know it, you will have started a domino effect in which a widening circle of people indirectly connected to you is following your lead.

Second, join a pro-European campaign group. Open Britain, Best for Britain and the European Movement are the leading organisations, backed by experienced politicians and businessmen and led by skilled campaigners and communicators. Donate, volunteer, participate in their social-media campaigns. Persuade them to combine their resources and work more effectively together.

Use social media wherever and whenever you can. Once again, follow the example of those who have campaigned for Britain to leave the EU: the online battlers who fight for Brexit and never seem to log out. In the run-up to the referendum, their tenacity clearly paid off. Research by the London School of Economics showed that Vote Leave and Leave.EU outperformed the official 'Stronger In' campaign on social media, reaching a wider audience and engaging in more relentless activity.[86] Further academic analysis has shown that twice as many

Brexit supporters were using Instagram and they were five times more active than Remain users,[87] while Leave supporters were also found to outnumber the Remain camp by seven to one on Twitter.

Why? LSE research suggests that 'Leave was able to draw on a deep well of arguments and pitches, honed over the years', while the campaign for Remain was 'largely from scratch, trying to find resonances among a public unaccustomed to hearing such views'. In other words, the emotive, chest-thumping cries of the Leave campaign drowned out the technical, economic arguments of the Remain camp. A familiar story, but one that was dramatically amplified by social media.

So, join groups and comment on pages on Facebook that you disagree with. Engage the opposition with argument. Identify individuals who are influencing discussions, and share or counter their views, depending on whether or not you agree with them. Find tweets or pages that are flagging up key events and make sure they reach a critical mass of people. Don't limit yourself to Facebook and Twitter, but get signed up to Instagram, Snapchat and any WhatsApp group that is participating in Brexit debates.

Tweet out the countless articles that show how damaging the Brexit vote has been for Britain. Share your positive experiences of being part of the EU, such as the ending of mobile-phone roaming charges, the EU rules which mean you can claim compensation on flights which are cancelled or delayed by more than three hours, or the care that you received from an NHS doctor or nurse who has come here to work from elsewhere in the EU. If you follow my advice and write to your MP, then post the response and encourage others to follow your lead. If you intend to join an anti-Brexit demonstration, then spread the word online.

It will make a difference. Even if you are a newspaper reader, always remember that for a significant – and growing – number of people, the Internet is the place to turn for news. More than 90 per cent of the UK's social-media users have a Facebook account, with the BBC now the only news media organisation in the UK that reaches more people through online news.[88] Little wonder that Dominic Cummings, the mastermind of the Vote Leave campaign, put 98 per cent of its money into digital adverts.[89] The young people who overwhelmingly voted to keep Britain in the UK are, as ever, ahead of the curve. A survey last year showed that 28 per cent of 18–24-year-olds state that social media is their main news source, compared with 24 per cent for television.

Third, work with a charity or voluntary organisation that you are already a member of. The Royal Society for Protection of Birds has more than a million members – way more than membership of the Conservatives, Labour and Lib Dems combined. The National Trust is even bigger: it has more than four million members. According to the Charity Commission, there are more than 160,000 third-sector bodies – that's charity and voluntary organisations – in the UK. More than 800,000 people work in the third sector. That's a ready-made army of allies and supporters waiting to be mobilised. Work with your group and make everyone demand to meet their MP and make him or her explain what Brexit means for the voluntary and charity sector's funding, support and values.

Fourth, think about what other networks you could mobilise, especially if you work in the public services. Teachers, police officers, firemen, nurses, doctors – Brexit affects everyone in many ways. If you are part of a wider union, make it work for you. Unite, Unison, the GMB, the FBU and other trade unions all called on their members to vote Remain in the EU. NASUWT, the teachers' union, has raised its concerns. So has the Royal College of Nursing. Manuel Cortes, the General Secretary of TSSA (the Transport Salaried Staffs' Association), has voiced what many are now thinking: 'If, as I suspect, staying within the EU is the best deal on offer in 2019, we should not deny voters the possibility of taking it.' The unions still wield big influence, not least over the Labour Party. So if you are a member of a union, then it's time to apply the pressure. Share your concerns and voice them.

Fifth, and finally, take to the streets: 23rd June 2018 marks the second anniversary of the referendum. It is a chance to make your unhappiness known on a national scale. Up and down the land, in every major city and town in Britain, the people who want a different future should assemble and protest. The protests should be coordinated and designed to culminate in a march down Whitehall to the Houses of Parliament. Cynics will remind you that the million people who protested against Tony Blair's decision to join the invasion of Iraq did not stop the bombs falling on Baghdad; that the bugle cries of the Countryside Alliance went unheard as fox-hunting was outlawed. Yet mass demonstrations can also help accelerate change. The millions of young people who voted in the referendum, and those now old enough to do so, should take to the streets – and social media – with placards declaring 'Not In My Name'. That would be impossible to ignore.

*

Assuming this pressure – on the political parties, on MPs, from more and more members of the public – starts to materialise in the next year or so, what would success look like?

The first, vital crunch point is most likely to come in the autumn of 2018. That is when it is widely expected that the outlines of a Brexit 'deal' will be presented to MPs ahead of the legal departure from the EU by Britain at the end of March 2019.

Whilst it is impossible to foresee exactly what will happen, it is safe to predict that any deal will fall far, far short of what the British people were promised at the referendum and what ministers have promised since. From NHS funding to lower immigration, from scientific research to red tape, from international investment to crime-fighting – on almost every conceivable count it should be relatively easy for MPs to demonstrate that what they are being offered by the government is both inferior to what the UK has, as a member of the EU, and to what everyone was promised by the Brexiteers.

This feeling of being let down, being sold a fudge, being asked to vote for a sleight of hand will only be exacerbated by the circumstances in which any 'deal' will finally materialise. For a start, there may be no deal at all, if the negotiations have broken down in complete acrimony – in which case, there is a profound risk that the Conservative Party will trigger a new election on an angry nationalistic platform, and market confidence in the UK economy will collapse. But even if a 'deal' is salvaged from the talks, it is highly likely that it will only happen at the fifty-ninth minute of the eleventh hour – no doubt very late at night, at a marathon summit of EU leaders – arrived at after much acrimony and, crucially, after the government has had to accept a series of humiliating climb-downs.

The likelihood of this happening is already evident in the conduct of the early parts of the Brexit talks: at almost every juncture the UK has had to give way to the EU, whether it be on the sequencing of the negotiations, the principle of paying significant sums to settle Britain's outstanding obligations to the EU or the likelihood that Britain will have to follow some European Court of Justice rulings after Brexit. The full weakness of Britain's negotiating hand will become starkly obvious by the autumn of 2018, if it is not already clear enough.

Furthermore, whilst there will no doubt be considerable detail to scrutinise on the 'divorce' elements of Brexit – issues touching on the operation of the Irish border, the rights of EU citizens, money, customs technology and procedures, pensions and staffing in Brussels, and so on – it is highly unlikely there will be fully fledged new arrangements in place governing the relationship between the UK and the EU in the future. Given that the government itself appears to have accepted that there will be a gradual transition period after the legal departure of Britain from the EU, it suggests that the detailed t's and i's of any final deal will be crossed and dotted many months – perhaps years – after MPs are being asked to vote.

In other words, MPs will be asked to give their consent in the autumn of 2018 to a Conservative government plan that will be rushed, late, surrounded in acrimony, weak and incomplete. In those circumstances, how could any independent-minded MP *not* reject the proposal before them? If the MP is a Brexiteer, they couldn't in all good conscience go along with something that clearly falls short of what they told their constituents they would get; and if the MP is a Remainer, they couldn't in all good conscience go along with something that confirms all their worst fears.

So if MPs, across party lines, were to signal that they were going to reject the government's proposal, what would happen then? A number of possibilities would arise. The government could, in a dramatic U-turn, announce that it was, after all, going to subject its package to another vote of the British people. It could, equally dramatically, trigger a general election, on the basis that it had lost the confidence of Parliament and needed to reassert itself by seeking a larger majority. Either of these two outcomes – another referendum or an election – would allow voters across the country to have their say again on the wisdom of proceeding with Brexit. For all the reasons set out in this book, and mindful of the acrimony that would no doubt arise once again, I believe that the British people would vote to change the judgement we arrived at in the Brexit referendum of June 2016 – especially because voters will, unlike then, be able to compare the promises made by Johnson, Farage, Gove et al. with the reality before them.

There are two further possible outcomes: the first, quite simply, is formal delay. The UK government could ask the EU for a decision – which will need to be taken unanimously by all twenty-seven member countries – to extend the deadline for the Brexit negotiations under the terms of Article 50. This will be widely regarded as a deeply humiliating thing to do, a British Prime Minister begging her/his counterparts for more time. Or, less humiliatingly and more informally, the EU could simply decree that it has 'stopped the clock' in the Brexit talks. It would have to do so in any event, if a new referendum or another general election were to occur, because no negotiations could proceed until these had been completed. More generally, the EU has a long tradition of stringing out difficult talks and negotiations, in the hope that time allows solutions to emerge. Internationally it happens, too – global trade talks within GATT and now the World Trade Organisation have always slipped several years beyond their original deadline. If there was to be some slippage in the timing of the Brexit talks, this would not only increase the chances of a change of government in the UK, but the current composition of the European Parliament and European Commission would also change after the summer of 2019. So any 'stopped clock' would almost inevitably lead to a longer delay than was initially anticipated, as new leaders took up their positions around the negotiating table.

This, in turn, might increase the chances of the EU itself evolving in a way (as described at the start of the book) that would be more amenable to Britain re-entering the EU fold at a later stage. It would be at this point – when the UK is still, in practice, functioning as a member state of the EU, even though it has passed the legal point of departure, or the legal departure date itself has been delayed – that cool heads and wisdom would be required to start putting Humpty Dumpty back together again.

Making Britain great again

SOME MIGHT ARGUE THAT we should simply turn the clock back to where we were on 22nd June 2016 and continue with our membership of the EU as before. I do not think such a return to the status quo ante is wise, or feasible. Those who believe Brexit is a mistake should not make the same high-handed error committed by the Brexiteers. After the referendum, they simply assumed that they could ignore the 48 per cent of voters who had voted the other way. But one half of the electorate cannot simply wish away the dreams and hopes of the other half. An accommodation must be found.

In a mature democracy, the winner simply cannot take it all. What the Brexiteers have sought to do since the referendum – disenfranchise and ignore more than sixteen million voters – is as absurd as if the Remain side had emerged victorious on the morning of 24th June 2016 and instantly announced that Britain would be joining the euro, signing up to the borderless Schengen Agreement and conscripting its soldiers into a new EU army.

Britain has been badly divided by the refer-endum, and we must now go forward in a way that helps to heal those wounds. After angrily stumbling out of the club in the early hours, it would be a bizarre act, having sobered up, to sneak back in past the bouncers and pretend that we were enjoying ourselves all along. Because we weren't. Many Britons were, and still are, deeply uncomfortable with our place in the EU.

I understand that unhappiness, much though I don't agree with it. Even the most passionate of Europhiles, myself included, accept that Europe must change, and that the people who voted to leave cannot be ignored. Ambivalence has been the consis-tent feature of Britain's membership of the EU since we joined the club in the early 1970s. If anything, it was perhaps surprising that as many as sixteen million people voted in favour of remaining. So I accept that the EU must look and feel different, if we are to stay a part of it. An impossible aim? Not in the slightest. As we saw in the first part of this book, over the last four decades Britain has repeatedly shown that it can shape the EU around its own values and needs and, with some imaginative thinking, can do so once again. More importantly, recent developments across the continent have left the EU with a renewed willingness to reshape itself for the twenty-first century.

So if Brexit is to be reversed, we have a duty to reflect the ambivalent feelings that Britain has felt from the moment we first joined what was then the European Economic Community in 1973. A new deal clearly has to respond to the worries and hopes of people right across the country. We must find a new accord, forge a new deal, in which Britain is neither a core member of the European Union nor stuck on the outside, looking in. With a combination of ingenuity and generosity, we can reach a settlement that represents all sides of the debate. This is, without doubt, the only sensible way forward.

David Davis, the man leading our negotiations with the EU, has admitted that the whole process will make the 'NASA moonshot look simple'. But he had his coordinates wrong from the start. Britain must keep itself within the orbit of the EU, rather than send itself hurtling into outer space where, before long, nobody will hear us call for help.

But while it's all very well talking about what we might want, time is short and we need to act fast. So much of Britain's approach to the Brexit process, from the pre-negotiation posturing to the sight of the Cabinet negotiating with itself, has been marked out by a sloth-like aversion to action. With so little concrete progress emerging from the negotiations so far, about the most interesting revelation has been that David Davis and Michel Barnier share a love of hiking. But where Barnier appears to have polished his walking boots, plotted his route and stocked up on energy bars, Davis is still struggling with the zip on his waterproof.

The formalisation of an EU of concentric circles – with Britain reintegrated into it at the appropriate level – needs to be a process that, unlike the negativity and inaction of the Brexit talks, is swift and purposeful.

So how to proceed? It should be a formal undertaking, initiated by the EU Heads of Government (including the British Prime Minister), but removed from the bungling hands of government ministers and elevated above party politics. A joint UK–EU Convention should be formed and handed the task of repositioning Britain in one of the outer rings of the EU's orbit. It should be co-chaired by serious and experienced figures from either side of the Channel, appointed to coordinate talks and sketch out a future arrangement.

Let me state, for the record, who I believe should represent Britain in these crucial talks. I can think of no better-qualified person than Sir John

Major, a highly respected former Prime Minister and a man with a detailed knowledge of operating at the very top level of British and European politics. Lord Adonis, a former minister in the Labour governments of Tony Blair and Gordon Brown, has already suggested that Sir John could play the role of 'honest broker', and I wholeheartedly agree. It was a role he played extremely well when, as Prime Minister, he laid the foundations for a lasting peace in Northern Ireland, as he found meaningful answers to one of the most complex questions in the history of the United Kingdom.

He hardly needs me to promote his credentials, but it is also worth noting that Sir John skilfully led Britain through the often tortuous negotiations that led to the signing of the Maastricht Treaty in 1992. The treaty marked a crucial step towards creating the EU as we know it today. But while he helped to shape the direction of European travel, he also fought hard for Britain, ensuring (with justification) that Britain stayed out of the embryonic euro-currency project while also ensuring (with less justification) that Britain opted out of the social chapter on workers' rights across the EU.

Whoever represents the European Union in these talks will inevitably be portrayed as an enemy – of the people perhaps? – by head-banging

Brexiteers and, of course, the *Daily Mail.* They will need a cool head and a thick skin. My nominee for the role may not thank me, but I know that his focus on the challenge will not waver, even if the Eurosceptic sections of the British press lose the plot. Mark Rutte, the Prime Minister of the Netherlands, is a self-confessed Anglophile and has described Britain as a 'beloved partner' of the EU. Any suggestion, as there no doubt would be, that Mr Rutte would relish giving Britain some form of Brexit punishment-beating would be totally inaccurate. He deeply regrets our decision to leave. He is one of the longest-serving Heads of Government of a founding EU member state, is widely respected across the continent and, in March 2017, secured a third term as Prime Minister after defeating a populist rival – the anti-Islam Geert Wilders – just as populism appeared to be on an unstoppable march. And if the Brexiteers needed further convincing, Rutte cites Winston Churchill as a role model and has described Margaret Thatcher as 'an icon in English and European politics' who 'improved and strengthened' Britain.[90]

Mark Rutte and Sir John Major, working in tandem, would make an experienced, formidable and, crucially, trusted partnership. Supported by a small, carefully selected team, they could work at speed.

European leaders should insist that the timescale for this Convention should be short, with the specific aim of bringing to an end the damaging uncertainty of the Brexit stalemate. Once Article 50's point-of-no-return has been successfully delayed or paused, then discussions must not drag on. With clear goals, careful preparation and goodwill from both sides, I see no reason why their work could not be completed within six months. The methodical, occasionally creaking bureaucratic machinery of Brussels is frequently accused of being in need of industrial amounts of WD-40. Perhaps the speed and efficiency of this Convention would demonstrate that the politics of Europe is more than capable of operating with slick efficiency, when needed.

And let's be clear about what needs to be done. This is not about tinkering at the edges or tweaking directives. This is not about signing off on more of the same. Instead it is a proposal to build on the current momentum towards a Europe of concentric circles and agree how Britain fits into its fundamental design. The reforms required for this new arrangement would involve treaty change and, accordingly, referenda in several EU member states to secure public support.

For now, the question is: how would this new European Union look, and where would Britain sit inside it? The Convention itself must decide which is the best way forward, and what works in practice, but from my discussions with leading EU politicians, I believe the following proposals are workable, affordable and, most crucially, desirable.

The core of a reformed EU would remain, as it is now, the economic and monetary integration of the eurozone, under the de facto leadership of a reinvigorated Franco-German duopoly. Emmanuel Macron is promoting proposals for the creation of new eurozone institutions – in effect, a eurozone Finance Minister and a central budget – accompanied by structural reform in France and elsewhere to enhance the eurozone's competitiveness; and an expectation that the eurozone's paymasters in Germany and the other surplus countries will underwrite the liabilities of the currency union. Britain will have no business to interfere in this 'inner core', other than an expectation that British taxpayers will not be asked to foot the bill for eurozone liabilities. This was a point already conceded in David Cameron's much-maligned 'renegotiation' package, prior to the Brexit referendum.

Britain would remain, as it is now, by far the largest EU country outside the eurozone. As now, it would remain a member of both the Customs Union and the Single Market, would abide by relevant rulings of the European Court of Justice and would continue to be a full participant in the Council of Ministers and the European Council. British MEPs would continue to be elected to the European Parliament.

Crucially, however, there would be some limits placed on the principle of freedom of movement. In truth, it is a principle that has always been much more susceptible to elastic interpretation by national authorities. In Belgium, the authorities are quick to deport EU citizens who do not work and cannot support themselves. The tiny principality of Liechtenstein participates in the Single Market, but legally imposes limits on immigration. Its entire population may be around the same size as Tonbridge, but there is nothing to say that we could not explore an approach based on similar lines. The German authorities, in an attempt to protect domestic pay deals, have restricted the use of temporary EU labour in construction and other sectors. In the UK, by contrast, we have a non-contributory benefits system, a particularly open labour market, unrestricted access to healthcare and no administrative residence checks. Many European politicians are baffled about why Brexiteers blame the rest of the EU for an approach to freedom of movement that is largely of our own design.

Following the referendum, European politicians were also baffled that the British government made no attempt even to explore whether the EU would be willing to open talks on reforming freedom of movement. EU leaders expected Theresa May to raise the issue, and they would have been willing to work towards a new deal. That she didn't even ask rather underlines the lack of imaginative thinking that has come to define her approach.

Why wouldn't the rest of the EU want to find a new accommodation? The other twenty-seven member states want to see the UK pursue the least economically disruptive Brexit possible. The British economy is, after all, equivalent in size to those of seventeen of the remaining EU member states.[91] And voters in many other member states share a wider, if not necessarily identical, concern about the movement of people into and within the EU. So they would, I am certain, offer a commitment to reform, in return for a sustainable solution to the 'British problem'. What would have been a *verboten* subject only a few years ago is now firmly up for debate, with Emmanuel Macron using his first interview as President of France to make clear that reform was essential. 'What did Brexit play on? On workers from eastern Europe who came to take British jobs. The defenders of the European Union lost because the British lower middle classes said: "Stop!"' Macron argued, adding: 'Extremes feed off imbalances like this.'

Furthermore, recent events have shown that substantive change is possible in the way freedom of movement is administered, even as the sacrosanct nature of the principle continues to be asserted. Though the former Prime Minister David Cameron found that the new limits he negotiated on the welfare benefits provided to EU citizens were not enough to appease the Eurosceptic obsessives in his party and the press, the wording of the agreement signed off by the EU Council in February 2016 merits a second look: 'If overriding reasons of public interest make it necessary, free movement of workers may be restricted by measures proportionate to the legitimate aim pursued.' It is a clear starting point from which to secure a new emergency brake mechanism, which would – crucially – be available to all EU member states. Such an arrangement would allow any EU government to impose work permits or quantitative restrictions, if it could demonstrate that it is experiencing exceptional inflows of EU workers over an extended period of time. Britain would, to borrow a phrase, be taking back control – and would be expected to apply this brake immediately after it came into effect.

Of course the art of negotiation is also, in large part, the art of compromise. So for Britain to secure reforms on freedom of movement and, in so doing, reposition itself in the outer ring of EU nations, it should in turn offer to increase its involvement in other aspects of pan-European cooperation where we have natural assets, and where there is a clear national interest to do so. In other words, the Major–Rutte package could include a two-way movement: less integration in some areas, notably freedom of movement; but more in others, notably foreign and defence cooperation.

There was more than a whiff of desperation about Theresa May's sharp-elbowed determination to be the first European leader to meet the newly elected President Trump. But if the trip taught her anything – other than the Donald's anxiety about walking down stairs – it was the painful realisation that the romance has gone out of the 'special relationship'. Under Trump's dogma of 'America First', an isolationist US can no longer be relied upon to throw its considerable military weight behind its allies. The painful reality, for those Brexiteers who thought the warm embrace of America would be Britain's reward for walking out on its EU partners, is this: with Donald Trump inclined to ratchet down US commitments to the security of the European continent, and with America turning to the Pacific rather than the Atlantic in pursuit of its core strategic interests, a new approach to European defence and foreign policy is essential. And the only way forward is *more* Europe, not less, with EU governments shouldering more of the responsibility to safeguard the security of our own continent. British involvement – bringing with it military and diplomatic clout that is unrivalled by any EU state other than France – would be both essential and desirable.

To calm the grinding teeth of jumpy Brexiteers, this does not mean the formation of an EU army. Deeper cooperation on defence means greater pooling of military research and hardware, increased policy coordination between Berlin, London and Paris, and unflinching support for the emerging foreign-policy machinery of the EU. There could be no more obvious example of how pooling our sovereignty is the way to increase our power.

The British offer must be bold and generous, not least because the default position of the European Union – and certainly of the European Parliament – for the price of re-entry will be the loss of the various exemptions and opt-outs that Britain has so skilfully amassed over the years. Across the EU our peculiarly à la carte arrangement is seen as complex and unfair, with Guy Verhofstadt, the Belgian MEP coordinating the European Parliament's response to Brexit, arguing that re-entry could not be on the same terms. 'Like *Alice in Wonderland*, not all the doors are the same,' he has warned. 'It will be a brand-new door, with a new Europe, a Europe without rebates, without complexity, with real powers and with unity.'

So the Convention I am proposing will need to approach its work with realism and humility, as well as speed. This will not sit easily with the aggressive John Bull triumphalism that runs through so much of British Eurosceptic rhetoric. Britain will need to appeal to European self-interest and ask that our friends and allies do not force the UK into a humiliating and politically impossible position. We are, after all, tectonically and geologically fated to be the closest of neighbours. We are geographically joined at the hip.

It is clear that Britain will find itself asking a lot of the European Union. But we offer much in return, too. The other twenty-seven member states are willing to listen and, I believe, to move swiftly and strike a new deal that will reflect Britain's unique position in Europe. We can take heart from the encouraging noises from across the continent. President Macron of France has said that the 'door is open', a phrase echoed by Wolfgang Schäuble, the German Finance Minister, who has noted that 'the British government has said they will stay with Brexit … if they wanted to change their decision, of course, they would find open doors'. Irish Prime Minister Leo Varadkar has also deployed the open-door analogy, while Jean-Claude Juncker, the President of the European Commission, has a more seafaring vision of reconciliation. 'I don't like Brexit because I would like to be in the same boat as the British,' Juncker noted, before adding: 'The day will come when the British will re-enter the boat, I hope.' And in June 2017 Donald Tusk, the President of the European Council, put it rather more poetically when he lifted the lyrics of a famous John Lennon song. When asked if Britain might avoid Brexit, Tusk said with a wistful smile, 'You may say I am a dreamer, but I am not the only one.'

Conclusion

THE SEVENTEEN MILLION VOTERS who ticked the 'Leave' box had many reasons for doing so. From the facts available to them, and from the arguments they heard, they knew exactly what they were doing and should never be told otherwise. But they did not know they were being lied to. They were not aware that wealthy individuals with personal motives were skewing the national debate. They had no way of knowing, then, that what they hoped Brexit would bring would not happen, now. They didn't know that prices would rise or that public services would suffer. They do now.

For all the one-word answers in TV interviews about whether Brexit meant ripping up our Single Market membership or quitting the Customs Union, nobody was ever presented with an official manifesto for leaving the European Union. The victors of the referendum did not agree then – and still do not agree today – what Brexit actually means in practice. Instead we were left with a series of media stunts and soundbites on which to base a decision with the most enormous consequences for Britain's future. It is not a future that I want for this country or for my children. It is not what young people – who have to carry the burden of the consequences of Brexit – want, either.

Now that we can see what Brexit really means, why wouldn't we change our minds? Don't let anyone tell you that we can't. It is not too embarrassing to stop now. Never let anyone tell you that you are not entitled to have a better future than the one on offer. None of that is remotely true. We change our minds every day of our lives. We weigh up the situation and choose again. We reflect on what went wrong and try to do things differently. It is our right. It is *your* right.

Our MPs, so often vilified and ridiculed, can change Britain's future if they want to. With your help and pressure, they can do the right thing when the big decisions have to be made. You can help make them braver and bolder. The will of the people is not like a snapshot photo: once taken, never changed. It is a living, breathing combination of millions of people's needs, fears and dreams. And the will of the people *is* changing. The moment people realise they are free to take back control of their own future, and not be trapped by a wafer-thin vote based on lies and misrepresentation, then MPs will be emboldened to think again, too.

Of course there will be complexities in changing course – but, as this book has sought to explain, all routes away from Brexit are better and easier, in the long run, than the implications of Brexit itself. Crucially, it is now obvious that it is simply impossible to soften austerity – yet alone 'end' it – whilst proceeding with Brexit. The British public is, understandably, weary of the hard slog we have had to endure since the terrible financial crash in 2008. Brexit will only extend the pain.

We will need to reach out to our European neighbours and friends, having tested their patience and bewildered them profoundly. It will take time to rebuild the trust and amity which the Brexiteers have so casually thrown away. But, in the end, a simple truth will prevail: we are condemned by history and geography to be allies, neighbours and friends sharing the same space, the same seas, the same continent and the same values.

The EU itself is not a fixed thing. It changes all the time. Many of its greatest achievements and reforms were championed by Britain in the past. It has an elastic capacity to accommodate huge differences between different countries under one EU roof. That versatility can help, once more, to reincorporate the UK within the EU, but on a more settled basis – not within the inner core of the EU, but not cast out to the political wilderness, either. An accommodation, most especially on the vexed issue of freedom of movement, can be found as the EU develops into an ever more distinct union of 'concentric circles'. There is a future for us in that reformed Union, if we are prepared to grasp it.

Brexit does not have to be hard or soft, rough or smooth, clean or messy, or even red, white and blue.

In fact, Brexit does not have to mean Brexit at all.

Appendix A

Dear Jeremy,

As a Labour voter and a new member of your party, I was thrilled that your uplifting and inspiring message was heard by so many people at the last election. Thank you.

However, I remain concerned by Labour's stance on Brexit. The morning after the election you declared that people voted for you because they were 'voting for hope for the future'. That's true. But for millions of us — the majority of Labour voters, in fact — that is a future inside the European Union. It is certainly not a future outside the Single Market or the Customs Union — even if we stay inside them temporarily for the next few years. As I am sure you know, making ourselves poorer by going ahead with Brexit will make your mission to end austerity all the more difficult. I simply don't understand why you seem to be endorsing the government's position, when that is exactly what I thought I was voting to stop?

You may argue that the 'will of the people' commands you to do so but, as I am sure you know from many political battles over the years, politics should not just be about listening to one side of the argument.

You always insist that you are the type of politician who will listen to everyone, not least because, as you yourself said, 'leadership is listening'. So I hope that you will listen to the millions of Labour voters who put their trust in you on 8th June and are now deeply unsettled by the approach to Brexit that you have endorsed. This is not what I, and many people like me, thought I was voting for. Will you change your position, or should I change my vote at the next general election?

I look forward to hearing from you.

Yours sincerely,
A. Voter

Appendix B

Dear Prime Minister,

As a new member of the Conservative Party, the general-election result came as something of a surprise to me – as I'm sure it did to you, too.

I wonder if it has caused you to reflect on the way you have responded to the referendum result? You insisted that Brexit means Brexit. You declared that Britain had no choice but to leave the Single Market, the Customs Union and the jurisdiction of the European Court of Justice. You said it had to be this way, because the will of the people said so. I would argue that the difficult night you endured on 8th June suggests that the will of the people is not entirely supportive of your approach, wouldn't you?

You have since said that you have the 'humility' to 'listen to the message we got from people at the election', but I see no sign of that. Why are you determined to persevere with Brexit when you yourself campaigned against it? You will, perhaps, say because the will of the people commands you to do so. Well, Prime Minister, they also elected you, albeit narrowly, to lead them. You saw at the ballot box that the people do not want a hard Brexit; quite possibly they no longer want Brexit at all. Why won't you listen to the will of the people and do the right thing for Britain?

I look forward to hearing from you.

Yours sincerely,
A. Voter

Notes

1. David Davis speech, 'Europe: It's Time to Decide', 2012
2. Margaret Thatcher, Speech opening the Single Market, Lancaster House, London, 18th April 1988
3. HM Treasury, *European Union Finances 2016*
4. G. Gotev, 'UK Reimbursed in Excess of €111 Billion by EU since 1985', www.euractiv.com, 23rd May 2016
5. Eurostat
6. Office for National Statistics, 'Long-Term International Migration'
7. Office for National Statistics
8. https://fullfact.org/immigration/immigration-and-jobs-labour-market-effects-immigration/
9. C. Dustmann and T. Frattini, 'The Fiscal Effects of Immigration to the UK', *The Economic Journal*, November 2014
10. 'The Impact of EU Enlargement on Migration Flows', Home Office Online Report, 25/03 (2003)
11. As reported on *Newsnight*, BBC2, 21st January 2017
12. Mario Draghi, President of the European Central Bank, announced in July 2012 that he was 'prepared to do whatever it takes' to save the eurozone economy. The ECB subsequently provided eurozone banks with more than €1tn of liquidity, and purchased more than €2tn of government and corporate bonds (*Financial Times*, 'Mario Draghi's "Whatever it Takes" Outcome in 3 Charts', 25th July 2017).

13. P. Carrell and M. Rose, 'Merkel and Macron Agree to Draw up Roadmap to Deeper EU Integration', www.reuters.co.uk, 15th May 2017

14. A. Robert, 'Macron Outlines Plans for Multi-speed Europe', www.euractiv.com, 3rd March 2017

15. European Commission Fact Sheet, 'EU–Turkey Statement: Questions and Answers', 19th March 2016

16. J. Pisani-Ferry, N. Rottgen, A. Sapir, P. Tucker and, G. Wolff, 'Europe after Brexit: A Proposal for a Continental Partnership', www.bruegel.org, 29th August 2016

17. *White Paper on the Future of Europe*, European Commission paper, published 1st March 2017

18. A. Robert, 'Macron Outlines Plans for Multi-speed Europe', www.euractiv.com, 3rd March 2017

19. A. Banks, tweet sent on 4th December 2016

20. Nigel Farage in a speech on 24th June 2016

21. www.statisticsauthority.gov.uk, 23rd May 2016

22. Dominic Cummings, 'How the Brexit Referendum was Won', blogs.spectator.co.uk, 9th January 2017

23. Office of Budget Responsibility, *Economic and Fiscal Outlook – November 2016*, 23rd November 2016

24. D. Boffey, 'Record Numbers of EU Nurses Quit NHS', *The Observer*, 18th March 2017

25. Nigel Farage speaking on *Good Morning Britain*, ITV, 24th June 2016

26. K. Ferguson, 'Environment Secretary Michael Gove Confirms European Fishing Boats Will Still Operate in British Waters After Brexit', www.mailonline.co.uk, 3rd August 2017

27. *Question Time*, BBC1, 23rd March 2017

28. *Enforcement and Dispute Resolution – a Future Partnership Paper*, Department for Exiting the European Union, 23rd August 2017

29. D. Cummings, tweeting from @odysseanproject, 3rd July 2017

30. H. Smit, *Weighing Up Future Food Security in the UK*, Rabobank, March 2017

31. 'Have Jam Today – It Will Be Too Expensive Tomorrow', http://www.express.co.uk, 17th January 2017

32. Historical exchange-rate data retrieved from xe.com

33. Office for National Statistics

34. See, for example, K. Allen, 'UK Faces Tightest Squeeze on Household Incomes for Five Years', *The Guardian*, 6th July 2017

35. T. Lang, E. Millstone, and T. Marsden, *A Food Brexit: Time to Get Real*, Science Policy Research Unit, July 2017

36. E. Kellewe, 'Chateau Brexit? Average Price of Bottle of Wine Reaches Record High', *The Guardian*, 1st June 2017

37. Office for National Statistics

38. Office for National Statistics

39. I. Goodley and P. Inman, 'UK Comes Bottom of G7 Growth League as Canada Takes Lead', *The Guardian*, 31st May 2017

40. www.nfuonline.com, 22nd June 2016

41. Office for National Statistics

42. Society of Motor Manufacturers and Traders, July 2017

43. 'Japan's Message to the United Kingdom and the European Union', Ministry of Foreign Affairs, Japan, September 2016

44. *Rethink Manufacturing*, KPMG, February 2017

45. Home Secretary's Speech on the EU and our place in the world, Institute of Mechanical Engineers, 23rd April 2016

46. Such groups include the Cornerstone Group, the No Turning Back Group and the 92 Group

47. Such groups include the Bruges Group, the Euro Information Campaign, the European Foundation and Atlantic Bridge

48. See www.electoralcommission.org.uk, for donations made during the referendum campaign

49. A. MacAskill and A. Davies, '"Insecurity is Fantastic," Says Billionaire Funder of Brexit Campaign', Reuters, 11th May 2016

50. Stuart Wheeler, 'The EU and What the Conservatives Should Be Doing About It', speech to the Bruges Group, 30th April 2009

51. Peter Cruddas, 'Join Me in Reversing Two Decades of Misrule by Brussels', *Daily Telegraph*, 11th January 2014

52. Lord Farmer, 'A Brexit Will Be a "Bright New Beginning"', *Daily Telegraph*, 15th May 2016

53. Anthony Bamford, House of Lords, Hansard, 27th October 2016

54. H. Walker, 'Top Brexit Donor Pledges New Campaign to Oust Remainer MPs in General Election', www.express.co.uk, 14th May 2017

55. A. Pierce, 'Tycoon's £1m Brexit Boost', *Daily Mail*, 26th April 2016

56. K. Schofield, 'Arron Banks: £4,300 Loss is Price Worth Paying for Brexit', www.politicshome.com, 16th April 2017

57. Right Honourable Lord Justice Leveson, *An Inquiry into the Culture, Practices and Ethics of the Press*, The Stationery Office, London, November 2012

58. Richard Desmond made this comment while appearing on *The Wright Stuff*, Channel 5, 7th July 2015

59. A. Hagan, 'Who's the Real Cunt?', *London Review of Books*, Vol. 39, No.11, 1st June 2017

60. Paul Dacre, 'Why is the Left Obsessed by the *Daily Mail*?', *The Guardian*, 12th October 2013

61. T. Adams, 'Is the Editor of the *Daily Mail* the Most Dangerous Man in Britain?', *The Observer*, 14th May 2017

62. C. Neilan, 'Business Leaders to Push David Davis for Clarity Tomorrow at Chevening Meeting', *City A.M.*, 6th July 2017

63. Such groups include the Heritage Foundation, the Gatestone Institute and the David Horowitz Freedom Center

64. L. Kaufman, 'Breitbart News Network Plans Global Expansion', www.nytimes.com, 16th February 2014

65. J. Lester Feder, 'This is How Steve Bannon Sees the Entire World', www.buzzfeed.com, 15th November 2016

66. For the full transcript of the interview with Donald Trump, see www.thetimes.co.uk, 16th January 2017

67. J. Pickard and J. Garrahan, 'Rupert Murdoch Secretly Sat in on Interview with Donald Trump', *Financial Times*, 9th February 2017

68. International Monetary Fund (IMF) figures

69. Jeremy Hunt and Greg Clark, letter to the *Financial Times*, 5th July 2017

70. Ed Vaizey and Rachel Reeves, 'Why We Must Save Vital Nuclear Treaty with our Allies in the EU', *Sunday Telegraph*, 8th July 2017

71. Ipsos Mori, Lord Ashcroft polls and YouGov

72. A. Aftab, 'EU Referendum: UK Result Would Have Been Remain Had Votes Been Allowed at 16, Survey Finds', www.independent.co.uk, 24th June 2016

73. C. Barnard and A. Ludlow, *Unravelling and Reimagining the UK's Relationship with the EU: Public Engagement about Brexit in the East of England*, University of Cambridge and UK in a Changing Europe, May 2017

74. 'How Britain Voted', Ipsos-Mori survey

75. A. Asthana, 'Big Majority of Labour Members "Want UK to Stay in Single Market"', *The Guardian*, 17th July 2017

76. Survation survey, 2nd July 2017

77. *The Observer*/Opinium survey, 19th August 2017

78. YouGov survey, 19th August 2017

79. I. Silvera, 'Owen Paterson: EU Cannot Ignore Pro-Brexit Parties Winning 85% of the Vote', www.ibtimes.co.uk, 12th June 2017

80. Nigel Farage, 'The Great Brexit Betrayal Has Begun: The Tories Have Sold Out the British People – Now Even

Jeremy Corbyn Has a Tougher Stance', *Daily Telegraph*, 25th July 2017

81. H. Mance and M. Lindsay, 'Majority of New Conservative MPs Backed UK to Remain in EU', *Financial Times*, 23rd June 2017
82. Rachel Sylvester, 'It's Still Europe That Could Rip the Tories Apart', *The Times*, 25th July 2017
83. www.esrcpartymembersproject.org
84. P. Goodman, 'Over Three-Quarters of Party Members Support the Hard Brexit Option Recently Backed by Davis', www.conservativehome.com, 7th September 2016
85. P. Goodman, 'Jacob Rees-Mogg Tops Our Next Leader Survey of Party Members', www.conservativehome.com, 5th September 2017
86. A. Matsuo and K. Benoit, 'More Positive, Assertive and Forward-Looking: How Leave won Twitter', www.lse.ac.uk
87. V. Polonski, 'Impact of Social Media on the Outcome of the EU Referendum', www.referendumanalysis.eu
88. 'Where Do People Get Their News?', Oxford University research, 30th May 2017
89. M. Ward, 'Facebook Becomes Key Tool in Parties' Political Message', www.bbc.co.uk, 2nd June 2017
90. http://www.dutchnews.nl, 13th April 2013
91. IMF figures

Acknowledgements

WHILST THIS IS A short book, it has benefited hugely from long hours of help from others. Will Hammond, my editor, and Stuart Williams at The Bodley Head not only encouraged me to write it in the first place but provided such astute guidance on how I should marshal my disorganised thoughts. And Vicky Booth, Tim Colbourne and Sam Macrory at Open Reason gave invaluable support, tips and criticisms every step of the way. I owe Sam Macrory a particular debt of gratitude. He was a constant source of history, facts and anecdote – combined with a keen eye for the right turn of phrase – without whom it would have been impossible to bring this argument against the folly that is Brexit to life.